RF-8A Crusader fighters fly over Task Group 10.1 ship formation, dropping flash bombs in salute to President Kennedy, aboard USS *Oriskany* (CVA-34). (U.S. Naval Institute photo archive)

CONTENTS

Cover photo: An aerial side view of two U.S. Navy RF-8A Crusader reconnaissance aircraft of VFP-63 flying in formation. (U.S. Naval Institute photo archive)

Library of Congress Cataloging-in-Publication Data is available.

ISBN: 978-1-68247-990-2 (print)

ISBN: 979-8-89241-014-4 (eBook)

An F-8 Crusader pilot captures his own plane's shadow while recording a North Vietnamese gunboat ablaze from hits made by a Navy strike aircraft. (U.S. Naval Institute photo archive)

INTRODUCTION

In the historiography of American fighter airplanes, the Crusader first appears in the mid-20th century as a transitional aircraft. From inception to fleet introduction, the F8U bridged the gap from the earliest-generation turbojets of the Korean War to the wave of jet-powered fighter designs debuting in the late 1950s. The culmination of Korean War–era experience in airframe, materials, and electronics, the Crusader design was tailored to a class of dual-spooled afterburning engines that reached maturity in the mid-1950s. It was the last of a breed of true dogfighters, clinging to 20-mm cannons cued by pulse radar for ranging that would give way to newer designs with pulse-doppler radar, multiperson crew, multiengine, and missile-only armament by the end of the decade.

Yet, for naval aviation, the Crusader was hugely transformational. Having been relegated to close air support in Korea, naval aviation lacked the swept-wing performance brought to the fight over the Yalu by more capable Air Force fighters. Parity with the Air Force in fighter performance by shipboard aircraft had been achieved in the latter days of World War II, but by the end of the Korean War performance of the latter had stalled with the introduction of turbojets and swept wings. The newer technologies were initially viewed as inimical to carrier operations. The slow turbine-engine spool time and the lift-dumping character of swept wings at high angle of attack only aggravated the hazards of carrier approach and arrested landing. The service was ceding fighter dominance to the Air Force and, critically, forfeiting relevance in national defense planning while losing credibility with appropriators in the halls of Congress.

The Navy had emerged from the intense interservice scrum in the late 1940s off balance without a clear role in the nation's nuclear force, only to find its footing again when aircraft carriers held the line off Korea. By the time of the armistice that ended Korean combat in 1953, the Navy had two *Forrestal*-class supercarriers under construction, with plans for more. That year, the Air Force first flew the F-100 Super Sabre, achieving supersonic speed in level flight. The Navy inched forward. Flight decks in 1953 were still populated with straight-wing Panthers and Banshees, powered by anemic, first-generation Westinghouse and Pratt & Whitney turbojet engines. The J57 engine powering the Air Force's Super Sabre notched a leap forward in turbojet design and performance. It showed much greater thrust to be possible without a corresponding increase in fuel consumption or weight by upping the overall compressor pressure ratio. The engine won for Pratt & Whitney the Collier Trophy in 1952. The new turbojet allowed the Super Sabre to reach unprecedented speed and its own Collier award the following year. The J57 was ready and available for the Navy's next look at a high-performance carrier-based fighter.

The Vought Aircraft Company and Pratt & Whitney enjoyed a long-standing business relationship and a history with naval aviation that had begun in 1926. That year Vought ordered two hundred new Wasp engines to power the Navy's first Corsair, the O2U-1. In 1929 Vought and Pratt were allied corporately under the same holding company, the United Aircraft and Transport Corporation, remaining associated even after the holding company was broken up in an antitrust action. The two companies remained in close proximity physically, occupying adjacent factories in East Hartford, Connecticut. For the next decade all Vought's airplanes destined for Navy service were powered by Pratt & Whitney Wasp or Twin Wasp engines. Only when the need for factory floor space necessitated a move in 1939 by Vought to Stratford, Connecticut, fifty miles away did the plants separate; even then, close cooperation continued. In 1939, Pratt & Whitney introduced its phenomenal 2,000-horsepower Double Wasp engine, the R-2800. The R-2800 was the obvious choice for a new-design Navy fighter that drew on the best creative energies of what was now the Chance Vought Aircraft Company. Vought's design inventiveness wrapped the R-2800 in a slim, compact, and highly efficient aerodynamic form that would be flown by Navy and Marine Corps aviators to great effect in World War II—the indomitable F4U Corsair.

Fifteen years later, the challenge for Chance Vought was resuscitating the company's historical creative energy—specifically, harnessing the impressive new turbojet powerplant from Pratt & Whitney in an airframe that could negotiate the very tight and unforgiving tolerances of carrier landings. Vought's aerodynamicists, in an encore of inventive genius, laid down a sleek, slender fuselage mounting a high wing—swept at forty-two degrees and notched for high-speed stability, a low unit horizontal tail to minimize pitch-up, and a yawning intake under the nose. The company's designers conceived a variable-incidence wing to assure cockpit visibility over the nose despite the high-wing setting, with leading- and trailing-edge droops to enhance lift and control in the landing configuration. In combination, these features gave the Crusader eye-watering up-and-away performance and, equally, the best possible optimization for approach and landing on the carrier. The F8U Crusader brought naval aviation into the supersonic age. It was the first truly supersonic fighter to see widespread deployment in the majority of frontline Navy fighter squadrons throughout the late 1950s and early 1960s—and its maker was awarded its own Collier Trophy for conception, design, and development of the first operational aircraft capable of speeds exceeding 1,000 miles an hour.

In total, Vought produced 1,266 Crusaders, most of those filling out the inventories of the 71 Navy and Marine squadrons that operated the Crusader over its lifetime in active and reserve service. Navy fighter squadrons operated the airplane from March 1957 until its final carrier deployment in 1976, when in February Cdr. Jack Hamilton, commanding VF-194, made the last arrested landing of a Crusader gunfighter aboard USS *Oriskany*. Marines operated both the gunfighter and photoreconnaissance versions of the Crusader from late 1957 until late 1968. The photo-reconnaissance Crusader was flown by Navy reservists until finally retired in January 1987, at which point the Philippine air force and French navy were still flying their Crusaders. The airplane served with distinction in the Vietnam War, downing 18 enemy jets in aerial combat for a loss of just three. Eighty-four more Crusaders were lost to direct enemy action and another 517 were considered operational losses from 1964 through 1972.

When I set out to document the history of the F-8 Crusader it became immediately apparent that the canon is replete with works on the subject, some quite good. Most could be cataloged as design and development histories on the one hand or Vietnam war stories on the other. In the former category, the best is certainly William Spidle's *Vought F-8 Crusader*. Steve Pace has also produced a very good history of its development, *Vought's F-8 Crusader*. The best examination of a Crusader model not chosen for production by Tommy Thomason, *Vought F8U-3 Crusader III*. The earliest and most comprehensive treatment of Crusader history was that of Barrett Tillman, still the dean of naval aviation history, his *MiG Master*.

In the genre of operational histories, Peter Mersky has been the most prolific, with at least three titles;

F-8 Crusader Units of the Vietnam War, *F-8 Crusader versus MiG-17*, and *RF-8 Crusader Units over Cuba and Vietnam* rank among the best. Peter Davies contributed similar work with *F-8 Crusader: Vietnam 1963–1973*. Adm. Paul Gillcrist edited the most complete collection of pilot experiences in the airplane with *Crusader: Last of the Gunfighters*. Also, a number of shorter theses have joined the collection. Of these, the best analyses of the Crusader's wartime performance are Michael Weaver's "An Examination of the F-8 Crusader through Archival Sources" and Louis Gundlach's "The Last of the Gunfighter: F-8 Crusader over North Vietnam."

While these works form collectively an extensive archive of Crusader lore, each focuses narrowly on a single aspect of Crusader history. None, save Barrett Tillman's *MiG Master*, plumb the Crusader's history from inception through sunset, and his does not do it in a highly pictorial manner. This book takes the reader from the earliest Vought design formulations to the poignant retirement celebration of the last French Crusader squadron, touching along the way on the most important operational aspects of the aircraft's service life. Personal recollections of Crusader pilots are quoted only to underscore a trait or attribute of the airplane itself. Where this work departs from earlier studies is that it presents a deeper look at the F-8 Crusader in an image-heavy, magazine-style format accessible to scholars, enthusiasts, and general readers alike.

Much is owed to the publishing group at Naval Institute Press, including Jack Russell in Marketing, and the superb editorial team that includes, in Acquisitions, Steve Catalano and Jessica Sparks; in Production, Brennan Knight and Pel Boyer; and in Design, Kelly Oaks.

I am grateful for the assistance rendered by Patrizia Nava, senior curator at the University of Texas–Dallas archives, where the Vought Company records are held. My thanks go also to Cathie Barrington, president of the Vought Heritage Foundation, and to Roger Stites of the foundation for sharing a superb collection of photographs. At the National Archives and Records Administration, thanks are due to Lori Norris, Jacob Haywood, and Nathaniel Patch in Textual Records and to Cecilia Figliuolo and Todd Crumley in the Still Picture Branch. At the Emil Buehler Library in the National Naval Aviation Museum, thanks go to archivist Jared Galloway and, for his unstinting support, to volunteer archivist Capt. Robert Thomas, USN (Ret.). Appreciation is expressed to Kate Igoe, David Schwartz, and Amara Pugens in the Archives Branch of the Smithsonian National Air and Space Museum. and to Matt Proietta, Photo Section librarian at the Naval History and Heritage Command. Gratitude is also owed to Tommy Thomason for sharing his very well-informed insight on the flight-testing process.

I am indebted to former naval aviators—most of whom flew the F-8—for their contributions: Cdr. Curt Dosé, USN (Ret.), for sharing his father's logbook entries; Capt. J. Michael Welch, USN (Ret.), for his explanation of Project Shoehorn; Capt. Charles Klusmann, USN (Ret.), for his recollections of the shootdown of his RF-8A and his subsequent capture and escape; Capt. Larry "Hoss" Pearson, USN (Ret.), for F-8 mission-payload details; Capt. Robert "Raz" Rasmussen, USN (Ret.), for his helpful commentary on F-8 carrier landings; former lieutenant and F-8 driver Robert Miottel, for his harrowing memories of early F-8 landings; Diane Duffy, widow of Capt. Denis Duffy, USN (Ret.), for graciously sharing his logbook entries; Capt. Ray "Playboy" Slingerland, USN (Ret.), for his recollections of East Coast gunnery exercises; Cdr. Jerry "Biter" Arbiter, USN (Ret.), for his helpful explanations of the F-8 landing pattern as seen from the LSO platform; to Capt. R. Charles "Flash" Schroeder, USN (Ret.), for his recollections of the Crusader gunnery pattern; to Cdr. Richard "Hot Dog" Brown, USN (Ret.), for insights into east coast Crusader operations and to former lieutenant Morrie Lewis for sharing his superb photo collection.

Most profound thanks go to a small group of former F-8 drivers who were always available, who shared their F-8 experiences and personal photos, and who reviewed early excerpts from this text. They include former lieutenant Joseph Shea, Capt. William "Striker" Switzer, USN (Ret.), Cdr. Steve "SAM" Marinshaw, USN (Ret.), and Capt. Dave "Gator" Cowles, USN (Ret.). Captain Cowles, president of the Crusader Association, rates particular mention for his helpful sponsorship and guidance and for introductions to the organization's membership.

RESTORING A PROUD HERITAGE

Vought's first advertisement went nationwide in major weeklies within months of the historic first flight. (Vought Aircraft Co. Collection, Univ. of Texas at Dallas)

Vought chief test pilot John Konrad grasped a handhold and raised his left foot to the boarding ladder of a brawny, low-slung XF8U-1 experimental prototype, pulled himself over the cockpit rail, and eased into the seat. The motions were by now familiar, but from this perch, on this day, he would coax the big jet into the air for the first time. The moment had arrived after months of poring over cockpit layout, schematics, and test points. In preceding days the pace had grown more frenetic (though never rushed), with taxi tests, engine runs, and the mental rehearsal of the test plan and how he would respond to in-flight system aberrations or failures. The day before, Konrad and his backup pilot, Harry Brackett, had met with base operations staff for a flight plan briefing. The Muroc airfield environment was well known to Konrad—he had graduated from Air Force Test Pilot School on this site five years before—but never had he flown from the dry lake an airplane with as much raw power and performance.

In the minutes before sliding into the cockpit, Konrad arrived on the edge of flight line in the back of a company sedan with Paul Thayer, vice president for sales, and their boss, John McGuyrt, chief of flight test—the latter two both former chief test pilots for Vought with close calls recorded in their flight logbooks. Thayer had deadsticked the F6U Pirate onto a golf course near the Naval Air Test Center (NATC) Patuxent River, in Maryland, and McGuyrt had ejected from a wildly gyrating and spinning F7U Cutlass. The conversation was hushed and reassuring, looking ahead to the flight test program but ending with a stern reminder not to stay with the airplane too long if ejection was warranted. Konrad appeared all the more confident and relaxed as he stepped out of the sedan to the good wishes of his colleagues. Vought's future viability much depended on a successful XF8U-1 flight today. For the Navy, a successful flight meant its gamble on Vought's design would prove well placed, obviating the need to continue investing in upgrades to less-capable airframes. Those thoughts receded now as Konrad became absorbed in the pretaxi checklist on his kneeboard test card.

VOUGHT'S PERILOUS POSTWAR TRANSITION

The great industrialization of American aeronautic business in the 1940s transformed how airplanes were designed and built. Piston-powered aircraft were taken to the limit of development during the war, and production capacity swelled beyond anything conceived prior to 7 December 1941. Exponential growth to meet wartime demands created, by the end of the war, the scale needed to harness a new wave of technology. With scale came more investment in research and development (R&D). Well-run, innovative companies like Lockheed and North American had proven adept during the war at organizing breakthrough designs and production processes to field fighter aircraft that are recalled today as world-class: the P-38 Lightning and the P-51 Mustang. For the Navy, Grumman and Vought too had created outstanding shipboard fighters: the F6F Hellcat and F4U Corsair. Lesser names in the gallery of wartime producers—Douglas and McDonnell—did not yet have first-rank reputations as producers of fighter aircraft for the Navy but hoped to gain a solid footing for postwar growth.

Chief test pilot John Konrad on the boarding step of the XF8U-1 at Edwards Air Force Base. (Vought Heritage Foundation)

With the end of the war, though, industry confronted a dynamic technological upheaval brought on by the emergence of two new technologies in particular: turbojet engines and swept wings. Some companies ably managed the transition. Some that thrived in wartime production struggled to build viable paths forward in the new supersonic age. The Chance Vought Aircraft Company, despite its reputation for cutting-edge design with the Corsair and efficient mass production of over eight thousand Corsairs during the war, was failing to make the transition.

Turbojets and swept wings were, in the main, products of a highly evolved German wartime R&D regime. Once German data were disseminated in the United States after the war, the U.S. Air Force, in particular, spurred their adoption in its fighter designs. The U.S. Navy was more reticent. Swept wings required higher speeds on approach to an aircraft carrier, and early turbojets lacked the instantaneous thrust needed for waveoff after a missed arrestment on the flight deck, critical requirements for safe operations in the carrier environment.

Naval aviation, in hopes of not being left behind in these transformative years, did make measured steps toward modernization. The World War II landings at Tarawa were still in the planning stage when the Navy invited McDonnell to develop the FD-1 Phantom, a proof-of-concept fighter powered by the domestically developed Westinghouse turbojet. The Phantom proved a lackluster performer and saw only limited deployment after the war. The Navy's first attempt to capitalize on lessons from the FD-1 came before the war ended, when it let contracts for a "Carrier-Based Jet Fighter" in 1944. North American submitted the XFJ-1, McDonnell the XF2D-1, and Vought the XF6U-1—all straight-wing, jet-powered designs. The XF6U-1 did not display the imagination of earlier Vought designs. It was simple and uncomplicated—straight wings extending from a tube-like fuselage that enclosed an anemic and unreliable Westinghouse J34 turbojet. It served the purpose of familiarizing the company with turbojets but did little to ingratiate Vought with Navy evaluators. Severe departure (i.e., from controlled flight) characteristics and a tendency to "Dutch roll" (simultaneously yaw and rock) at high speed made every flight a calculated risk. The Navy chief test pilot, Cdr. Fred Trapnell, noted, "Throttle limitations to protect the engine only accentuated the airplane's lack of adequate power."[1] Vought engineered a fix by incorporating an afterburner, making the XF6U-1 the first Navy jet to feature this sort of thrust augmentation. In the first test flight it was discovered that the heat of the afterburner incinerated the empennage, or tail assembly, a structure built of Vought's proprietary balsa sandwich material. The response, to wrap the entire empennage in a stainless-steel case, only made the thrust-to-weight problem worse.

The next wave of Navy fighter advances was prompted when the Bureau of Aeronautics (BuAer)

The Pirate was followed by the F7U Cutlass, a radically different aircraft vehicle but woefully underpowered in its first iteration, the F7U-1. Vought followed up with the F7U-3, an improvement but still a complicated design that still suffered from inadequate thrust and only further tarnished Vought's reputation with BuAer. (U.S. Naval Institute photo archive)

issued Outline Specification (OS) 105 for a "Carrier-borne Day Fighter" immediately after the war. Vought's creative energies reemerged with a very radical swept-wing, tailless F7U-1 Cutlass, a design greatly influenced by the former chief designer of the German Messerschmitt company, Woldemar Voigt, now a Vought consultant, who drew heavily on his wartime Me P.1111 fighter concept. Again, however, engine performance was not up to the power demands of the air vehicle, and the F7U-1 did not enter a long production run. This was a clear setback: "The Cutlass was a fighter that Vought hoped would be the jet equivalent of its F4U Corsair."[2]

Three years passed, and the bureau again instigated the next leap in fighter design, issuing OS 113 for an "Escort/Interceptor Fighter." Vought answered the solicitation with its F7U-3, an upgrade of the Cutlass with a more durable airframe almost a third larger than the original. Problems surfaced immediately with flight control hydraulics and landing gear. The original J35 engine without afterburner was replaced by two Westinghouse afterburning J46s, but the airplane was dismayingly underpowered. The F7U-3 went into production and outfitted several Navy fighter squadrons, but disappointing performance did nothing to improve Vought's sinking reputation with BuAer. Project Cutlass test pilot and future Mercury astronaut Lt. Wally Schirra wryly noted, "The company soon became '*Chancy* Vought' to us, for in our judgment the Cutlass was an accident looking for a place to happen, a widow maker."[3] Of the more than three hundred Cutlasses built, fully one-quarter were destroyed in accidents, claiming twenty-five pilots before it was pulled from service. The Cutlass served as valuable learning experience in designing a swept wing, afterburning jet fighter, but it almost irretrievably squandered the reputation and prestige with the Navy that Vought had earned during the war with the F4U. By 1952 Corsair production was ending, and prospects now appeared very uncertain for the company continuing as a prime source of premier fighters.

THE CHANCE VOUGHT AIRCRAFT COMPANY RALLIES

Vought culture embodied a resilience and grit that reflected the heritage of its new Texas home. Company leaders seized on the next design opportunity being formulated by the Navy as the best bet for reviving a glorious past. Informal contacts by Vought with Navy counterparts in July 1952 provided some insight as to the service's thinking on a new day fighter—something that was light in weight, low in cost, and capable of a maximum speed of about Mach 1.0, but with performance not superior to that obtainable without an afterburner. In fact, the Navy was inclined to assess a penalty for space reservations to accommodate a future engine retrofit with afterburning power. If Vought's experience with the F4U, F6U, and F7U had taught anything it was that there could be no substitute for the highest possible performance, and Vought made that point emphatically at a presentation to the Navy later in July. Outline Specification 130 appeared in September 1952, announcing the Navy's desired parameters for a "Supersonic Day Fighter," whose primary mission would be to "maintain air superiority in daylight fair weather, both over friendly task forces and over hostile target areas during the period of task force strikes when the enemy will mount large numbers of aircraft."[4]

The September draft detail spec preserved language consistent with BuAer's original thinking to limit performance to 1.0 Mach. This was owing to insistence by the Chief of Naval Operations (CNO) staff that 1.0 Mach was adequate, considering the advantages that could be reaped from smaller size, lighter weight, and lower cost. By November, however, an amendment appeared that responded to Vought's insistence at the July presentation on opening the design space to the highest achievable performance, an accommodation due in part to the departure of the project officer on the CNO staff who had favored more modest performance specs.[5]

The amended OS-130 called for an increase in maximum speed from Mach 1.0 to 1.2, compatibility with an afterburning engine, low initial cost, ease of maintenance, and reliability and versatility in air-to-air combat. Vought's assistant chief engineer and proposal design lead, Russ Clark, met in November with the BuAer's VF (Fighter) Design Branch Head, Cdr. Syd Sherby, and his incoming relief, Cdr. Ralph Weymouth. There he learned that the wording of OS-130 was, in their view, sufficiently broad to permit at least two submissions from every bidder, implying a minimal-compliance design and a growth airplane.[6] Also revealed in those discussions was that the release was imminent of another, second amendment to OS-130 that, on one hand, imposed acceleration limits for catapulting and arresting until the new angled-deck modifications to *Essex*-class aircraft carriers proved viable, but on the other hand now permitted an augmented thrust engine.

Changes to Vought's wind-tunnel models were already in train that featured more wing area, high-lift devices, and the use of edge droop as ailerons. Conceptual layouts of different configurations persuaded the proposal team that two concepts clearly offered the best all-around designs to meet and or exceed the requirement.[7] This view was codified in "design philosophy" guidance issued by Vought's Engineering Department that steered internal consideration to, first, the smallest possible airplane with the smallest-thrust engine that met the design objectives, and second, the smallest possible airplane with the highest-thrust engine available to meet, and in most cases exceed, the design objectives. The Engineering Department defined those objectives as

- Maximum speed at 35,000 feet at military power (nonafterburner) of Mach 1.0
- Maximum speed at 35,000 feet at combat power (afterburning) of Mach 1.3 to Mach 1.5
- Potential growth speed at 35,000 feet at combat power of Mach 1.5 to Mach 1.7
- Ceiling at military power (no afterburning) greater than 48,000 feet
- Radius of action 300 nautical miles with normal load on internal fuel
- Takeoff, landing, and waveoff at military power (no afterburning)
- Spotting of 25 airplanes in 200 feet of deck
- Approach speed at 1.2 of minimum speed, no greater than 130 knots

And, thanks in large part to Vought's insistence with the Navy, design flexibility was permitted to accommodate powerplant upgrades.[8]

OUTLINE SPECIFICATION 130 COMPETITION

Wartime necessity was the impetus for broadly diffusing aeronautics technology and production capacity in the United States in the 1940s. The specter of the Cold War now stoked an interest in preserving a "deep bench" of aircraft designers and builders. Companies that had earned favor with the Navy during the war for their designs and efficient manufacturing practices now had to show themselves capable of mastering the new technologies. Chance Vought Aircraft Company was not alone in its pursuit of the Navy's Supersonic Day Fighter.

In one sense, the cycle of continuous progress in airframe and propulsion for higher speed and higher ceiling had reached its apogee. The next cycle, which would focus more on radar, fire control, and avionics was still a few years away. In 1952 and '53 the Navy was besieged with proposals, both unsolicited offerings and responses to outline specifications that sought to herd industry toward particular needs. Even as OS-130 was getting its first exposure to industry, Grumman was courting the Navy with an advanced version of the F9F Cougar that retuned the fuselage with "coke-bottle" indentations to minimize "wave drag" at transonic or supersonic speeds as predicted by the "area rule." Grumman had also upgraded the powerplant to an afterburning J65, a concept known internally at the company as the G-98. The Navy was interested enough to order three prototypes independently of the OS-130 competition. Grumman's strategy appeared to be to secure Navy funding for a flying prototype outside the competitive proposal that might serve as a risk-reducing surrogate, an inside track to a "directed buy." It nearly worked—Grumman's concept would evolve into the F11F Tiger, which appeared for a short time in the fleet.

Other companies were preparing multiple designs in response to OS-130. Nine companies, including Grumman, all with multiple options for wing sweep and powerplant, submitted altogether twenty-one separate design concepts. Most proposed the AN/APG-34 fire-control radar and some combination of 20-mm guns and several dozen two-inch rockets. Among those companies, Douglas tried to cover as many contingencies as possible with four variations of its Model 652, all derivative of the F4D Skyray design, with thinner wings and higher fineness ratios. The first iteration of the Model 652 was submitted outside of OS-130, and the Navy, intrigued by its promised performance, approved the build of five examples as F5D Skylancers. For their OS-130 response Douglas developed three additional concepts similar to the F5D, all with highly swept delta wings and "elevons" (controlling both roll and pitch) but with different engines, ranging from the J57 to

The F6U Pirate represented Vought's first experience with the design and production of turbojet-powered fighters. It was a poor performer and did not impress the Bureau of Aeronautics. (U.S. Naval Institute photo archive)

the Rolls-Royce Avon, with and without afterburner. Douglas estimated that its scaled-down 652A powered by an afterburning Rolls Royce Avon engine could reach Mach 1.41 at 35,000 feet. In the end, Douglas' F5D Skylancer failed to circumvent OS-130, owing to a very unfavorable set of flight tests at Patuxent River by future Mercury astronaut Alan Shepard.

Northrop followed a similar approach, submitting four variations of its N-94 design based on a tailless delta wing with cambered leading edge: a baseline N-94 variant with a larger engine, N-94A with smaller engine, N-94B with larger wing, and N-94C with larger, repositioned wing. Northrop intimated a top speed of Mach 1.3 at 35,000 feet for its concept powered by a J57-P-11.

For its part, North American, with orders already in hand for the J65-powered FJ-3 Fury, focused on a near-complete redesign of the Fury for OS-130 that moved the inlets to the side and adopted an 11-degree variable-incidence wing to improve pilot visibility and handling on carrier approach. North American's resulting F2J concept, powered by the J57, promised to be one of the most capable performers in the competition, attaining an estimated top speed of Mach 1.51.

Lockheed prepared a navalized version of its F-104 Starfighter then under consideration by the Air Force. Finally, TEMCO, a new entrant in the field, designed for a smaller, T-tailed, delta-winged, J57-powered airplane without afterburner.[9]

At Vought, minimal-compliance and growth concepts were drafted with similar arrangements and aerodynamic features but different powerplants. Vought's V-384 configuration would use the Wright J65W-(TJ31B3) engine, designed to just meet the specification threshold, which resulted in an airplane slightly smaller than the growth configuration. The V-383 concept, using the Pratt & Whitney J57-P-(JT3N) engine, yielded the smallest and simplest airplane that could be designed around the highest-thrust engine available under the amended OS-130 specification.[10]

VOUGHT'S PROPOSED MODEL V-383

Several design features with Vought's V-383 stand out in a concept that, in aggregate, yielded an airplane that was superior to all the OS-130 competitors. This was especially the case in a carrier flight deck environment and in up-and-away performance. A two-position variable-incidence wing contributed to a low-slung fuselage profile that permitted

- With shorter landing gear, easy access for pilot ingress and egress and for maintenance and servicing
- With the wing raised, catapult launch without the need for exotic ramps or any dynamic rotation
- Lower height for the nose-gear drop on arrestment, reducing nose gear loads
- Good pilot visibility over the nose on approach while preserving a faired windshield and canopy, and
- A high wing arrangement providing ample clearance for wing-mounted stores.

A careful evaluation of wind tunnel tests convinced Vought designers to add to the wing leading edge a distinctive notch, or sawtooth extension, that improved longitudinal stability at high speeds and directional stability at low speeds, and also increased available g's for maneuvering before onset of buffeting by 25 percent.

Wing leading-edge droop improved lateral control for landing when the leading edge drooped 20 degrees automatically on raising the variable-incidence wing. More efficient cruise was achieved when the full leading edge drooped 5 degrees and more effective combat maneuvering above 2 g's when the inboard droop moved to zero while the outboard leading-edge droop remained at 5 degrees. Wind tunnel tests confirmed that with the outer wing drooped 5 degrees, top speed could be improved by 0.1 Mach.

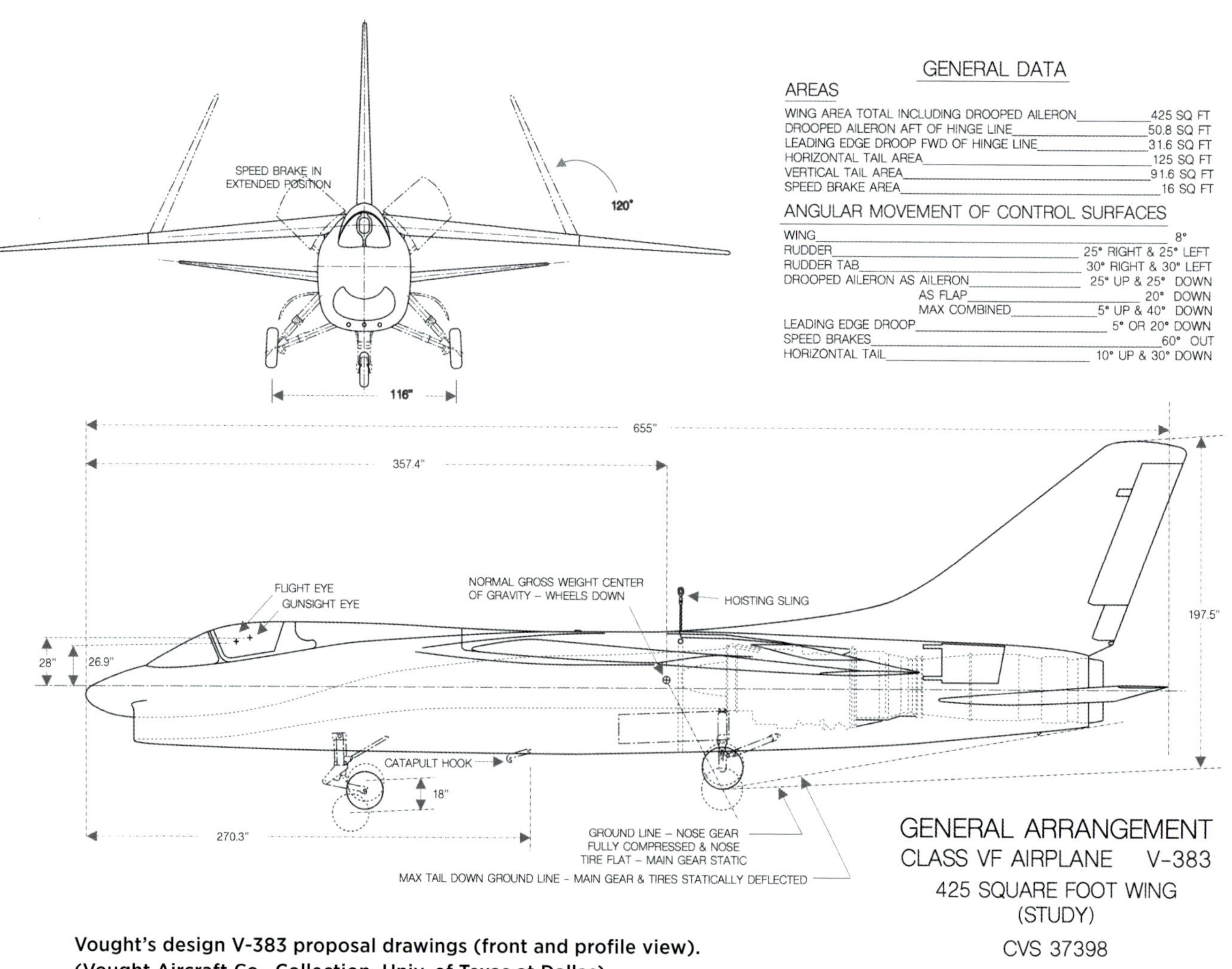

Vought's design V-383 proposal drawings (front and profile view). (Vought Aircraft Co., Collection, Univ. of Texas at Dallas)

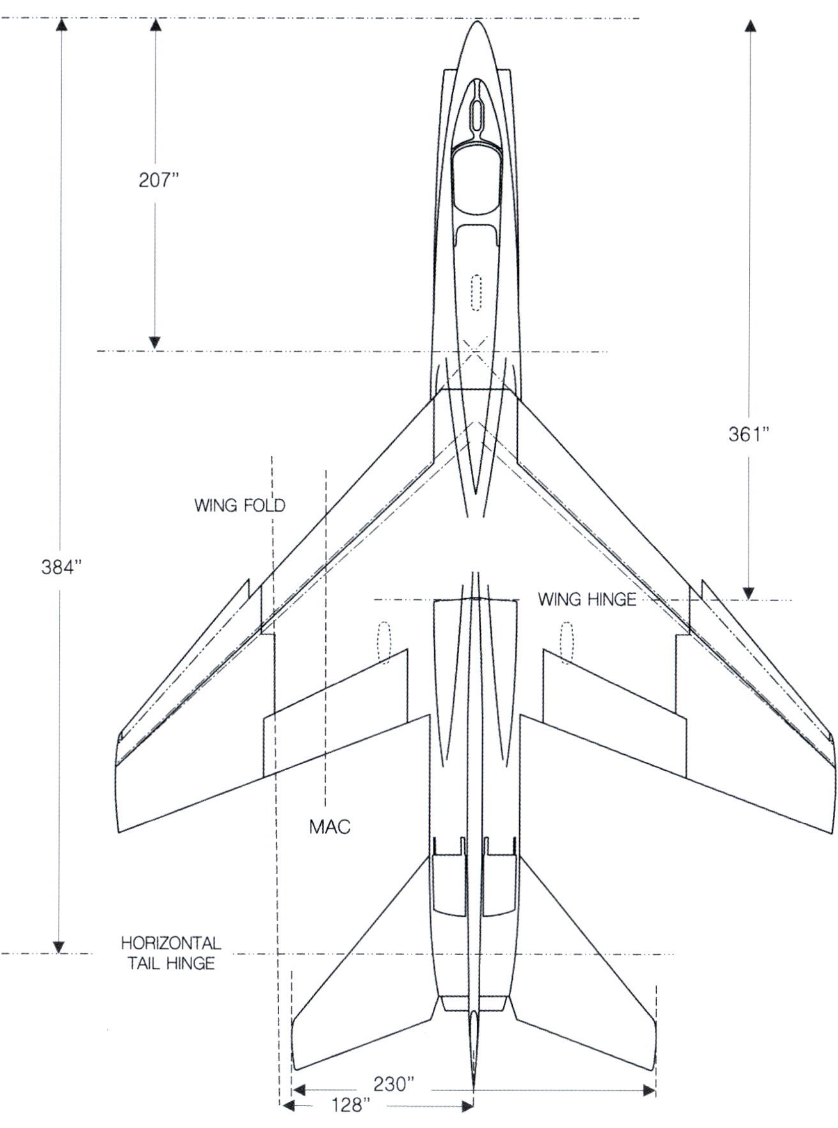

Vought's design V-383 proposal drawing (planform view). (Vought Aircraft Co., Collection, Univ. of Texas at Dallas)

Likewise, when the variable-incidence wing was raised and the trailing edge flap drooped automatically for reduced altitude on approach, lift modestly increased and lateral control improved. Even from the lowered position, the flap could be deflected with pilot input 20 degrees either way. This meant the pilot retained low- and high-speed roll control with the flap drooped. A unit horizontal, or "all-flying tail," is also linked to the wing incidence movement such that trim is adjusted automatically when wing incidence is changed.

Vought's design trade-offs clearly pointed to the Pratt & Whitney J57 powerplant from the BuAer-approved list. The most important requirements determining engine selection were radius of action, military power ceiling, and maximum speed at combat power, meaning afterburner. When plotted as available thrust versus powerplant weight (engine + fuel + fuel system), the J57-P-JT3N mapped to a very impressive thrust-to-weight ratio, the J57-P-11 at slightly less thrust but 1,000 pounds lighter. Possible substitutes for the J57 included the Allison J71 or the GE J73, but both came with lower performance. Assessing options for the J65-powered configuration, designers identified another engine in development that might have been a desirable retrofit for Vought's smaller V-384 concept with even better thrust-to-weight than the J57—the GE J79. Vought judged, however, that the greater fuel burn and larger intake ducts imposed by a J79 compromised overall performance. In any case, the J79 would not finish its qualification tests for another three years, much too late for the Navy's OS-130 timeline.

Design data and performance guarantees were sent to BuAer on 27 February 1953, followed two weeks later by cost data. Proposed aircraft performance for V-383 indicated a 2 percent increase in combat ceiling over threshold, to 49,8000 feet, and a 25 percent increase over the specified Mach 1.2. Vought's quoted price to BuAer for three experimental prototype airplanes and a static-test "article" (a nonflying surrogate used to test structural load limits) was $14,003,304 (slightly more than $160 million today), including a fixed fee of 3 percent.[11]

A CRITICAL WIN!

Jubilation in Grand Prairie, the company's Texas home, was the order of the day when on 19 May 1953 Vought received a BuAer message announcing, "[Y]our proposed design . . . has been selected for award of a contract."[12] The assistant bureau chief for R&D, Rear Adm. Robert S. Hatcher, noted that Vought's V-383 was "the most flexible design from a loading standpoint, carrying internal fuel for the 400 nautical-mile radius with

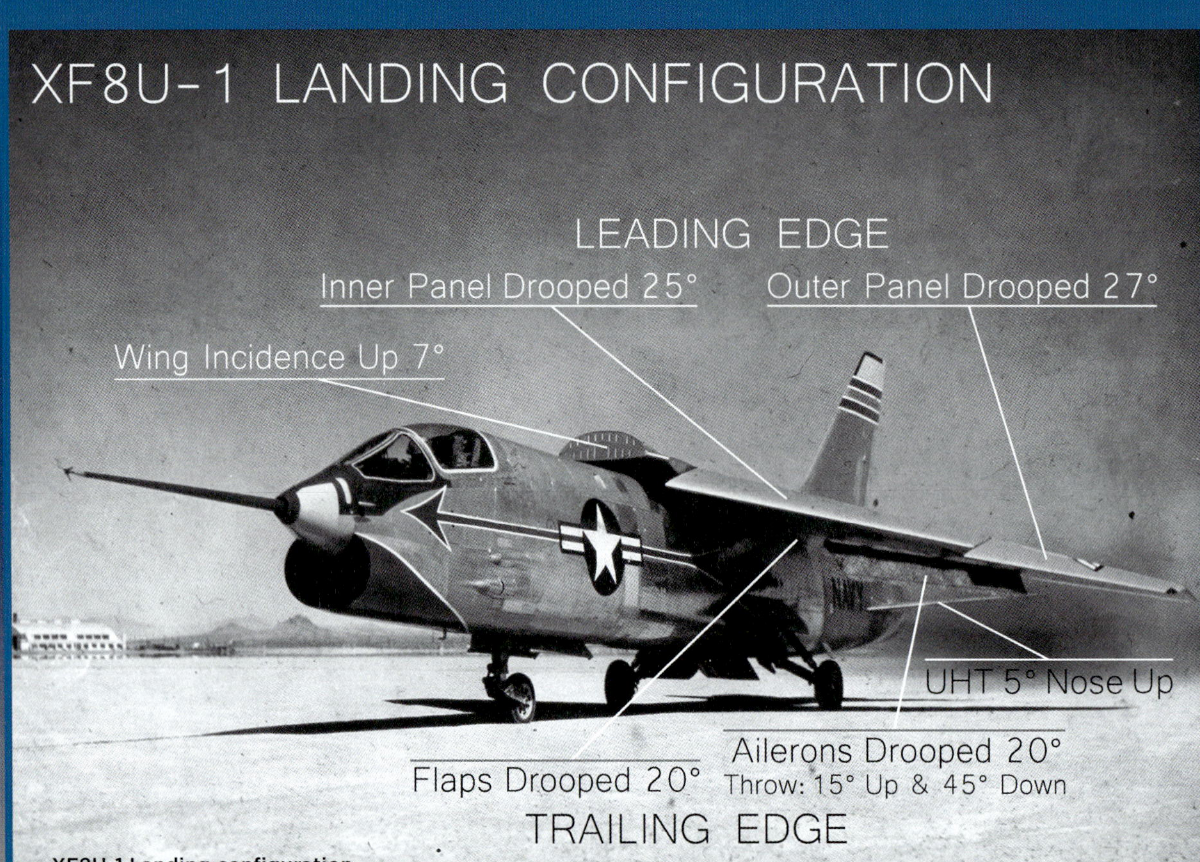

XF8U-1 Landing configuration. (Vought Heritage Foundation)

XF8U-1 mockup, left front. (NARA)

XF8U-1 takes flight from Muroc on 25 March 1955 with John Konrad at the controls. (Vought Heritage Foundation)

XF8U-1 readied for flight at Muroc. (Vought Heritage Foundation)

both guns and rockets, and for the 500 nautical-mile radius with either guns or rockets. The performance is as good as is its carrier suitability."[13] Hatcher added in summation, "[T]he Chance Vought design appear[s] to represent the best compromise between the many conflicting requirements, and as a swept-wing, tailed aircraft it filled a void in the overall VF (Navy Day Fighter) program."[14]

The company was advised to treat the notice as informational only, not to be acted on pending negotiations on price and on detailed performance specifications. Even so, the Vought rank and file interpreted the message as a sure indication that the company was about to return to its former preeminence. Engineering was given the go-ahead to proceed with design work. Detail Specification for the XF8U-1 was negotiated and on 3 June 1953 was signed. Interestingly, the document's armament section prescribed three 20-mm guns and/or 60 two-inch internally carried rockets with space provision for four Sparrow 2 missiles. Ultimately, this specification would give way to four 20-mm guns without provision for Sparrow missile mounts. The rocket pack would be retained in the first production blocks but removed in later series production. More significantly, the Detail Specification was the catalyst for production planning for an initial lot of 316 F8U-1 aircraft, numbers of them for testing and operational development.

A "letter of intent" received on 30 June ordered three airplanes, designated XF8U-1, for experimentation and one for static testing. Vought's "scope of effort" was altered slightly by BuAer in October, eliminating the third experimental prototype in favor of a representative likeness, or "tactile mockup." Already, work on the mockup had yielded a highly useful facsimile, ready for internal company review by the end of August, preparatory to a Navy review a month later. The Navy meeting convened in Grand Prairie in September 1953 with a Mock-Up Review Board of more than two dozen technical advisors, nearly all representing BuAer functional disciplines. They supported the oversight work of the Review Board Committee, a five-person panel of highly qualified naval aviators and senior civilian engineers from BuAer. Chaired by Ralph Weymouth, the Mock-Up Review Board recommended numerous "tweaks," such as adding a wing fuel dump, improving pilot rear vision, and providing greater clearance from the canopy when grasping the ejection-seat face curtain. All were cataloged and prioritized, and most were adopted as Engineering Change Proposals for Vought to carry out. The board's recommendations were to be carried forward into the next iteration of the XF8U-1 Detail Specification, negotiated and issued in January 1954.

By December 1953, wind tunnel tests conducted primarily at the National Advisory Committee for Aeronautics (NACA) Langley Research Center in Virginia and Ames Research Center in California revealed unexpectedly high supersonic drag, poor directional stability at speed, barely acceptable maximum lift in a landing configuration, and excessive trim change required during speed-brake operation. "Coke-bottle" indentations to the fuselage midsection to reduce drag were examined but deferred to later consideration to minimize costly redesign and retooling. Several other options were investigated to address aerodynamic performance, resulting in a slenderized nose, a sharper inlet lip, and relocation of the speed brakes on the lower forward sidewall of the fuselage to a single brake on the bottom. Increases in outer-wing-panel leading-edge droop from 20 degrees to 30 and of center-section leading-edge droop extension from 20 degrees to 25 were recommended for improved longitudinal stability in the landing configuration.

More changes were coming based on continuing wind tunnel tests now being run at the transonic tunnel at Cornell University in New York and the slow-speed tunnel at the Massachusetts Institute of Technology. Aileron span and flap area were increased for better lift coefficient, and a 22-inch extended tail cone was incorporated in the No. 1 airplane. Structures testing was completed on the No. 1 airplane by February 1955, and preflight operations began around-the-clock to close out the remaining tests required before the first flight, which was to take place at Muroc Dry Lake (now Rogers Dry Lake) in Edwards Air Force Base (AFB), California. (Muroc had been chosen since runway extension at Naval Air Station [NAS] Dallas was not yet complete.) Fuel tests were completed on 1 March; the wing was removed from the No. 1 airplane, loaded on a flatbed truck, and started the next day. The following day the fuselage was loaded on an Air Force C-124 cargo plane and carried to Edwards to be mated again with the wing. Crews worked a split 24-hour shift to reassemble the airplane and complete system checks in time for the scheduled first flight on 25 March 1955.

THE HISTORIC FIRST FLIGHT!

Now, on the day, Konrad readied himself. With concurrence from the tower, he made one high-speed run down the runway accelerating to rotation speed to confirm that everything looked to be in working order. He returned to the downwind end of the runway, turned around, and positioned for his takeoff roll, making a radio check with the Vought telemetry van to confirm that contact was good and systems functioning and ready. One more scan of hydraulic readings, a check of emergency pitch trim, a look at the stabilator damper, and myriad other steps on the pretakeoff checklist confirmed that all was in readiness. Konrad leaned forward slightly for one last look left and right to verify that the wing folds were extended, wing incidence raised, and leading-edge flaps in takeoff droop. With a "wipeout" of the cockpit, moving flight controls in all directions to ensure they were free and not binding, he called for takeoff clearance.

The early afternoon temperature on the dry lake was slowly rising through 80 degrees under a near-cloudless sky, with winds steady at 10 mph from the south. With takeoff clearance Konrad advanced the throttle to a momentary pause at 80 percent on the engine tachometer, punching the timer on the instrument panel (just outboard of the lever that dropped the tailhook to start the second-hand sweeping to record elapsed time). He glanced to the lower left of the instrument panel to check engine pressure ratio and exhaust gas temperature, then scanned to the lower right to see that fuel flow looked normal. Now, releasing foot pressure on the brakes he advanced the throttle fully to the stop, or detent, then past it to engage the afterburner. The airplane accelerated straight and true, with no unintended drift to one side or the other. His scan dropped to the center-left of the instrument panel to look for airspeed. At 125 knots indicated airspeed he started a gentle pull-back on the stick, and the nosewheel lifted off.

To observers on the edge of the dry lake, the XF8U-1 appeared to emerge suddenly from the cloud of dust kicked up by the jet's exhaust. Acceleration now was brisk. Konrad was barely airborne when he reached for the gear handle, then immediately for the wing retraction lever on his left behind the throttle and the locking lever to hold it in place. He leveled off at 16,000 feet and pulled the throttle out of burner. When the airplane had slowed sufficiently, he dropped the

Observers gather to witness Konrad's first flight of the XF8U-1. Vought officials include (*left to right*): G. K. Johnson (materials manager), Russ Clark (assistant chief engineer and XF8U-1 development), Joe Silverman (quality control program management), Paul Thayer (sales manager and former chief test pilot), and Harold "Slats" Sallada (assistant to President Fred H. Detweiler and former BuAer chief). In uniform and cap, Cdr. Joe Rees (BuAer XF8U-1 project officer). Russ Clark (in fedora) was holder of the patent for the aircraft's design, along with XF8U-1 project engineer Lyman Josephs and Conrad Lau, XF8U-1 lead aerodynamicist. (Vought Heritage Foundation)

XF8U-1 No. 2 is prepared for flight from Carswell Air Force Base in Fort Worth on 11 June 1955. (Vought Heritage Foundation)

landing gear and raised the wing to put the XF8U-1 in the "dirty" (higher drag, for landing) configuration so as to check wing extension, leading- and trailing-edge droop, and slow-speed handling. Raising the gear and retracting the wing, he relit the afterburner to climb still higher. At 35,000 feet he leveled off, pulled out of burner, and checked high-speed handling. Satisfied, he now advanced the throttle past the detent to ignite the afterburner, watching the airspeed meter climb through 1.0 Mach, reaching 1.05 Mach.[15]

In 52 minutes of flight, a new threshold had been crossed in naval aviation. Never before had an airplane broken through 1.0 Mach on its very first flight. The exuberance at Vought at winning the Day Fighter design contract was now surpassed at this new record-shattering milestone, and with it the prospect of an enduring business base. On the XF8U-1's landing the occasion was saluted in a high-speed flyover by the chase plane, an Air Force F-100 piloted by Lt. Col. Pete Everest, head of flight testing at Edwards and at that time the world speed record holder in the F-100. Climbing down from the cockpit, Konrad turned to BuAer's XF8U-1 Project Officer, Cdr. Joe Rees, and said, "Well Joe, there's your new airplane." Rees just

smiled and answered, "She sure looks good!" In an open letter to Vought employees at the end of the week, the company president, Fred Detweiler, declared, "This is an event of great importance to our company. The day fighter is the first new airplane to be produced by Chance Vought since we separated from United Aircraft Corporation and it affords us an excellent opportunity to reestablish as a separate company the sound reputation which we have enjoyed in the past."[16]

The next day, the XF8U-1 entered into a dynamic flight test program to open up and explore the flight envelope and begin validation of flight and subsystems performance. On the whole, the initial test flights identified very few major modifications required to the configuration. After fiftey-six flights that extended into June, the No. 1 XF8U-1 was ready to turn over to the Navy. Early that month No. 2 airplane was ready for flight, but Vought could not count on availability of the C-124 a second time, so the airplane was hauled by flatbed truck the 35 miles from Hensley Field at Grand Prairie to Carswell AFB at Fort Worth. First flight for No. 2 occurred on 11 June 1955 at Carswell, after which it was ferried to Edwards Air Force Base on 15 June 1955 to join the No. 1 airplane for the flight test program.[17]

In August Vought's president, Fred Detweiler, announced to employees that after screening two hundred suggested names, the company's chairman, Charles McCarthy, had selected "Crusader" to be used in all future references to the day fighter. Advertising started the next month, reaching the aerospace trade via *Aviation Week* magazine in early September, followed by a broader public exposure in *Life*, *Time*, and *US News and World Report* in the weeks that followed.[18]

NOTES

1. Frederick M. Trapnell and Dana Trapnell Tibbits, *Harnessing the Sky* (Naval Institute Press, 2015), 164.

2. Trapnell and Tibbits.

3. Robert Bernier, "Forty Years Building a Dream," (Smithsonian National Air and Space Museum, Washington, DC), *Air and Space Quarterly*, 21 September 2022.

4. Chance Vought Aircraft, "Proposal Detail Specification, Navy Day Fighter (OS-130): Report 8978," 3 June 1953, Vought Aircraft Company Collection, University of Texas at Dallas.

5. Chance Vought Aircraft, "XF8U-1 & F8U-1 Program Synopsis: July 1952: December 1956," 1957, Vought Aircraft Company Collection, University of Texas at Dallas.

6. William D. Spidle, *Vought F-8 Crusader* (Specialty, 2017), 18.

7. Spidle, 19.

8. Vought Aircraft Company, "Navy Day Fighter Design Philosophy: Report 8699," 21 February 1952, Vought Aircraft Company Collection, University of Texas at Dallas, 4.

9. Tony Butler, *Early US Jet Fighters: Proposals, Projects and Prototypes* (Hikoki, 2013), 170–84.

10. "Navy Day Fighter Design Philosophy," 6.

11. Chance Vought Aircraft, "XF8U-1 Program History," 1958, Vought Aircraft Company Collection, University of Texas at Dallas.

12. Rear Adm. Thomas S. Combs, Bureau of Aeronautics [hereafter BuAer], Letter Aer-CT-3 (191400), 18 May 1953, National Archives and Records Administration [hereafter NARA] Record Group [hereafter RG] 72 box 404, College Park, MD.

13. Butler, 182.

14. Butler.

15. Steve Pace, *Vought's F-8 Crusader: Development and Testing, Foreign Users and F8U-3* (Steve Ginter, 1988), 2.

16. Vernon B. Hobart, "Navy Unveils Day Fighter," (Chance Vought Aircraft, Dallas, TX), *Chance Vought News*, 20 June 1955, Vought Aircraft Company Collection, University of Texas at Dallas.

17. Spidle, 61.

18. Vernon B. Hobart, "F8U Is Named Crusader," (Chance Vought Aircraft, Dallas, TX), *Chance Vought News,* August 1955, Vought Aircraft Company Collection, University of Texas at Dallas.

THE NAVY TAKES A SERIOUS LOOK

Early production line. (Vought Heritage Foundation)

Factory assembly of the preproduction airplanes followed the two XF8U-1 prototypes almost without interruption, at three per month initially, then eight per month. George Spangenberg, then head of the Evaluation Branch in BuAer, later remembered, "It was really concurrent from day one. It had all been planned that we let the first contract for two airplanes but then within the next year we bought five and then twelve and then twenty . . . to get a smooth production buildup. We bought enough experimental or early production airplanes to get the test flying done. If you have just two airplanes it takes forever. And if you do them as pure prototypes you've cut corners all through the thing and you don't have a representative sample."[1]

NAVY PRELIMINARY EVALUATION

Navy test pilots became directly involved with the XF8U-1s not long after the first flight in a formal step known as the Navy Preliminary Evaluation (NPE). Instituted in the late 1940s, NPE amounted to a schedule of airborne tests to give the Navy a hands-on "first look" at the aircraft, conducted in cooperation with, but independent of, the contractor. It produced a final technical report on the aircraft's suitability for its intended purpose before certification of the airplane for a more comprehensive final exam by the Navy's Board of Inspection and Survey—or more commonly, BIS trials. NPE was typically structured in progressive phases "(1) early definition of future operational capabilities, (2) a spotlighting of gross deficiencies which could inhibit combat effectiveness or safety of flight, and (3) a comprehensive assessment of developmental status to BuAer."[2]

Four functional divisions of the Naval Air Test Center (NATC) at Patuxent River in 1955 involved Navy and Marine test pilots in all aspects of initial aircraft testing for NPE and beyond: Flight Test, Service Test, Electronics Test, and Armament Test. In the Flight Test Division, new airplanes were "wrung out" not just to confirm contract compliance but to expand the aircraft's flight envelope and determine basic in-flight performance limits, such as service ceiling, climb rate, fuel consumption, and endurance. Cdr. Robert "Duke" Windsor was chief projects officer in Flight Test when the XF8U-1 was handed over to the Navy. Preliminary Evaluation started at Edwards AFB; Windsor and Marine major Lynn Helms from the Flight Test Division headed to the high desert with a test plan drafted by Helms. Windsor recalled, "We did all the stability control performance on all the new jets. I'd been back about two months when we went out to Edwards to test the newest one which was the F-8 Crusader. We did all the original flying on the F-8 Crusader."[3]

Windsor made the very first flight of the XF8U-1 for the Navy. Seventy-five percent of his flight was allocated to "power approach" (PA) mode, checking stability about all axes of flight for control and power response when, first, configuring for landing, then "cleaning up" the airplane for climb-out. The remainder of his time was in cruise (CR), changing power settings to reach predetermined speeds and economic cruise at different altitudes. Helms flew next, spending most of his flight time in cruise. Flight testing at this point involved the use of an Ames gauge to measure stick forces, a stopwatch to time certain maneuvers, and a kneeboard card with test points requested by the engineers. At the pull of a trigger, a bright light from behind the shoulder made it possible to record instrument readings for later data reduction by the engineers.

Both test pilots noted that overall flying-quality differences between PA and CR were far more exaggerated in the XF8U-1 than in other aircraft they had tested. The airplane wallowed excessively about all three directional axes, noticeably in PA configurations. Most disconcerting, though, was an extreme transient in the pitch axis at high speed, accompanied by severe oscillation about the longitudinal axis. Windsor experienced ever-increasing oscillating cycles from −1.9 to +5.7 g; if he let go of the stick, it ceased. At high Mach, both pilots also noted an increasing aileron "buzz." Vought engineers made changes to the wing incidence angle, modified ailerons, installed a wing center-section inboard flap to address the wallowing, and a wing center-section spoiler to arrest the oscillation about the longitudinal axis. Regrettably these fixes were not in place before the unanticipated lurch in pitch accompanied by roll oscillation destroyed the first preproduction model, killing Vought test pilot Harry Brackett, John Konrad's backup on the first flight. Neither were they fully incorporated before Marine major Jim Feliton joined Windsor and Helms in the third phase of NPE, at Grand Prairie. Feliton, on his first F8U-1 flight, was close to 1.0 Mach at 25,000 feet when uncommanded pitch excursions tore off the entire wing. Feliton broke his leg on the canopy during

F8U-1 is serviced adjacent to the island superstructure of the USS *Forrestal* (CVA 59) preparatory to carrier suitability trials by NATC test pilots. (Vought Heritage Foundation)

F8U-1 compatibility with the *Forrestal*'s elevator is checked. (Vought Heritage Foundation)

ejection but parachuted down without further injury. Phase 3 was terminated.

Phase 4 of NPE bore down on the oscillations. Vought's aerodynamics lead, Connie Lau, found a little-known company north of Dallas named Texas Instruments that was then making minute force-measuring instruments for oil drilling rigs and brought them in to build accelerometers in sealed containers only slightly larger than an aspirin. One was placed in the nose and one in the tail; their measurements signaled a control box that would, it was hoped, dampen flight controls to eliminate pilot-induced oscillations. It worked.[4] The final gripe, one that both Windsor and Helms insisted on addressing before they could clear the airplane for INSURV trials, was the need for a locking device for the wing in up or down position. Prompted in part by Feliton's experience, they wanted the wing locked at high torsion during high-Q rolls (rapid rotation about the longitudinal axis) at high g. Paul Thayer, former naval aviator and now Vought's chief test pilot and vice president for sales, heartily agreed. His concurrence made it happen quickly—the Crusader would have a wing locking handle.

Maj. John Glenn, who would become more famously connected to the Crusader and later as an astronaut, served as a project test pilot in Armament Test, evaluating fire control systems for the F8U-1. In one

F8U-1 in tension on the starboard catapult, ready for launch with NATC test pilot. (NARA)

of his flights, having done most of the supersonic gunfire points and moved into the low-altitude high-Q points at three thousand feet for the next firing, he encountered a rare but unsettling phenomenon with the Crusader's four 20-mm guns.

At high subsonic speed, Glenn depressed the stick-grip trigger, and his F8U-1 immediately made an uncommanded roll 90 degrees to the right. He tried retrimming the airplane, but the "normal" reading in aileron trim on the indicator was off by several points on the cockpit gauge. Slowing for an emergency landing, he discovered that the force of the uncommanded roll to the right only increased. The Crusader was still controllable at higher landing speed, so Glenn brought the airplane down for a longer landing run-out than usual. Once he had parked the aircraft and folded the wings, he could see that the wing structure from the leading edge of the tip back to the aileron was missing. Nineteen square feet of wing was simply gone. Further investigation by Vought engineers yielded the answer. The four cannons, as installed, were free-firing, each seeking its own individual natural fire rate, many hundred rounds per minute. Instruments revealed that all four guns had for a split second pulsed together and produced a destructive resonance, sending toward the wingtip a standing wave that flexed the outer wing and snapped it off. The fix was fairly easy: an interrupter cutout switch that would momentarily stop one gun from firing when the four guns arrived at that resonant frequency.[5]

Inevitably, when designs leave the drafting table to become physical flying hardware, anomalies are revealed in flight testing that could not have been anticipated. These sorts of testing "surprises" are not everyday occurrences, but these instances illustrate the value of early evaluation by experienced Navy and Marine test pilots to unearth them before less-experienced pilots in the fleet unsuspectingly encountered them. Glenn, in addition to his work with the F8U-1 weapons, would become increasingly involved with photographic configurations of the soon-to-be-defined F8U-1P.

Flight Test involved a Carrier Suitability Branch that, for the F8U-1, meant determining the aircraft's compatibility with steam catapults and arresting gear. Windsor, in addition to project tasks for expanding the envelope, was head of the Carrier Suitability Branch when it took up the F8U-1. "We started to get it ready to go aboard the carrier so being the boss, I made myself the project pilot for it. I did the first catapult shot and the first arrested landing in the Crusader."[6] For a first look at F8U-1 handling qualities on the flight deck—taxi, towing, parking, elevator compatibility—and initial carrier launch and recovery demonstrations, Windsor and his small team of Carrier Suitability test pilots took F8U-1 production airplane No. 3 aboard the USS *Forrestal* (CV 59) in April 1956. The Crusader was graded satisfactory in all shipboard handling demonstrations, with surprisingly little said about difficulties on approach flying to an on-speed arrestment.

The first six production airplanes were allocated to NPE for demonstration of structural integrity throughout a closely defined flight envelope, initial carrier suitability work, engine performance and responsiveness testing, demonstration of the fire control and armament system, and finally, in-flight validation of engineering change proposals that were beginning to accumulate and be incorporated from earlier test flights. Among the Navy's immediate-priority changes in this preliminary phase were an engine swap from the J57-P-11 to the J57-P-12 for a bump-up in thrust and faster spool-up; clearance of restrictions on the ram-air turbine for emergency electrical power; and installation of nose wheel steering to correct for sluggish turning with differential braking taxi. Beyond these, perhaps the more serious concerns were less-than-optimal roll rate and failure of the afterburner to relight and tendency to blow out. As testing progressed, changes were recommended and incorporated for external carriage of Sidewinder missiles (in lieu of Sparrow missiles) and for in-flight refueling. Vought designers settled on a refueling probe on the left-hand side of the upper fuselage, stowed in a faired blister, that on pilot selection articulated to the ready position in the airstream. Production F8U-1s from No. 66 on would receive the probe modification.[7]

Happily for Vought, which had the F8U-1 already in production in limited quantities, the Navy deemed performance adequate to the specification; area-rule changes to the outer mold line would not be required. Critically, however, area-rule changes that could improve fuselage contour for lower drag continued to be examined for the F8U-1P design. F8U-1 production airplane No. 1 made its initial flight just six months after the first flight of the XF8U-1 prototype. The first F8U-1P made its initial flight on 17 December 1956, a date no doubt chosen in commemoration of the Wright Brothers' first flight.

NATC test pilot and future astronaut Lt. Cdr. Alan Shepard flies an F8U-1 on final approach to Hensley Field, adjacent to the Vought factory, for instrumented tests of newly installed runway arresting gear. (ALAMY)

THE PHOTO RECONNAISSANCE CRUSADER: F8U-1P

Vought had learned the intricacies of airborne photography in the early 1940s, modifying its propeller-driven Corsairs with cameras for prestrike and poststrike target imaging. Photo Corsairs were still flying combat missions in the first two years of the Korean conflict, but they proved too slow and vulnerable to intense ground fire. Navy air groups began deploying to Korean waters with photo reconnaissance versions of the early jet fighters, the F9F-2P Panther and F2H-2P Banshee, flown mainly by detachments of Composite Squadron (VC) 61. Marine photographic squadron VMJ-1 deployed to airfields in Korea with the same reconnaissance jets. Those early straight-wing jets were nearing obsolescence at the end of the Korean conflict. However, experience more relevant for Vought was already being collected. Company "configurators" were at work designing a photo reconnaissance version of the F7U-3 Cutlass. By extending the Cutlass nose more than two feet and deleting the nose radar and the gun system, they could accommodate in the jet nine photographic windows and two primary camera racks, with the option for as many as five cameras. Only twelve versions were built, but the experience translated directly to "base-lining" the F8U-1P design.

Early in the F8U design process, in August 1953, Vought produced a proposal for a next increment of F8U-1 procurement that included two F8U-1P aircraft, with the forward fuselage reshaped to accommodate camera stations, windows, and night photo flare pods by removing the 20-mm guns and ammunition bay. Windows required flat surfaces to give the cameras distortion-free fields of view, which in turn required that the fuselage be squared off on the ventral and sidewall outer surfaces, then faired into the nose section, canopy, and fuselage forward of the main landing gear wheel well. The increased frontal area of the squared fuselage produced much more drag than was desired, limiting top speed. Here, the area rule, abandoned for the F8U-1, was crucial to achieving a more aerodynamic airplane; coking resulted in a distinctive hump on the top side of the fuselage behind the cockpit. The reshaped fuselage had the intended benefit of also submerging the refueling probe behind a flat fuselage sidewall, thereby eliminating the drag produced by the blister shape that was so prominent on the F8U-1.

The photo Crusader was designed with four camera stations. Station 1 was below the cockpit, a bulged teardrop shape with a faired-in slanted window that gave a forward-looking 16-mm movie camera an oblique view of the aircraft's flight path over the ground on ingress to and egress from a target area. The camera could be set before flight for a 10- or 25-degree depression angle. Stations 2 could accommodate a vertical camera, an individual 30-degree oblique camera mounting, or a trimetrogon arrangement for horizon-to-horizon coverage. Stations 3 and 4 could mount cameras for vertical imaging, various oblique angles, or night photography. Depression angle for these last two stations could be varied from the cockpit by the pilot, who could operate them using a trigger switch on the stick.

As originally configured, stations accommodated a mix of CAX-12 cameras to obtain vertical and oblique exposures. This allowed for post-flight stereographic interpretation of the topography. CAX-12s belonged to a new family of 70-mm aerial cameras designed to compensate for the higher speed of aircraft like the F8U-1P. The selection of cameras and their mountings could be adapted, in limited ways, to the needs of the mission, whether controlled by the pilot or in automatic mode.

A supplement to the F8U-1P Detail Specification in June 1956 outlined a typical mission for day reconnaissance that would mount a combination of camera equipment: Station 1, one forward oblique-aimed 16-mm camera with film and mounts; Station 2, three CAX-12 trimetrogon cameras; Stations 3 and 4 with CAX-12s, but K-17 cameras as an alternate. With more experience, hangar-deck crews could accommodate two cameras in Stations 3 and 4, giving oblique and vertical coverage.[8] In practice, as would become apparent, most Navy photo labs could not obtain the quality needed for successful interpretation using the CAX camera's 70-mm format. As a matter of operational necessity, the CAX-12 would eventually be replaced by a larger-format KA family of cameras.[9]

A window just behind the nose cone in front of the intake lip allowed the pilot to see his flight path on low-level ingress to a target area. This was helpful in lining up the approach for the camera run. The scan from that window was displayed on a cockpit viewfinder that replaced the radarscope in the upper center of the instrument panel. With a cockpit switch the pilot could overlay a drift line and grid marks to gauge his progress over terrain. Night photography missions required the use of flares carried in an upper fuselage compartment that formerly housed 20-mm ammunition canisters. An enlisted photographer's mate (PH) from the squadron embarked aboard the carrier would replace a light monitor inside the camera compartment meant

A viewfinder window under the nose, plainly visible here, remained a prominent feature of the photo version beginning with the F8U-1P through subsequent upgrades to the RF-8A and RF-8G. The viewfinder provided the pilot with a wide- or narrow-angle view of the area being photographed, with overlaid grid marks to determine picture-taking interval. Here, Lt. (jg) Morrie Lewis of VFP-63 prepares to strap into his RF-8 in 1964. (Morrie Lewis)

Vought's photo Cutlass, though never introduced operationally, added to Vought's understanding of the mission and configuration developed during World War II with 39 F4U Corsair photo versions—experience applicable to the F8U-1P. (ALAMY)

to suppress daylight reflection off the terrain. In its stead the enlisted photographer's mate mounted a flash detector that once airborne generated a pulse to fire the camera when it detected a flare ignition.

The photo Crusader also got the mockup treatment, but only a partial reconstruction of the forward fuselage. Navy and Marine evaluators thought this adequate to highlight the position of the camera bays and a typical camera loadout. The F8U-1P received its own Mock-Up Review Board in May 1955, twenty months after the F8U-1's. Among the participants was Major Glenn, representing NATC's Armament Division. Glenn was joined on the board by representatives from VC-61 and -62 and VMJ-2, all then still flying either the F9F-6P photo Cougar or F2H-2P photo Banshee. The prototype F8U-1P, built from the 32nd production F8U-1, made its first flight just 15 months after first flight of the No. 1 production F8U-1. The effect of reshaping the airplane with area rule for drag reduction was confirmed in early 1957 flight test in which the prototype F8U-1P was flown at 35,000 feet to Mach 1.426 in afterburner. In total, 144 photo reconnaissance versions of the Crusader would roll off the assembly line at Grand Prairie.

F8U-1P mockup. Over camera station No. 2, flare ejectors for night photography are seen where ammunition canisters in the gunfighter F8U would be located. (NARA)

F8U-1P mockup, right-hand side, showing camera configuration. (NARA)

F8U-1P mockup with ventral camera windows open. (NARA)

F8U-1P demonstrator takes flight with forward fuselage modifications to F8U-1. (Vought Heritage Foundation)

BOARD OF INSPECTION AND SURVEY

The INSURV Board was then, and is now, as an independent activity outside BuAer jurisdiction, reporting to the CNO. It does not have the in-house resources to conduct flight tests. BuAer delegated Air Development Squadron 3 (VX-3) to support INSURV trials using the next seven production airplanes. Four more production airplanes were sent to NATC at Pax River for various experimental flights, the next six to fleet introduction.[10]

In today's aircraft testing environment, Air Test and Evaluation Squadron 23 at NAS Patuxent River evaluates and tests flying qualities, performance, shipboard suitability, and mission system for tactical aircraft. In 1956, VX-3 performed those functions and in December of that year received the first of its new F8U-1s for evaluation in support of INSURV trials. VX-3 resided at NAS Atlantic City, New Jersey, and was commanded by Cdr. Robert G. "Bob" Dosé, an experienced fighter pilot who had led VF-12 during World War II, flying F6F Hellcats from the deck of the USS *Saratoga* (CV 3).

VX-3 took up its testing once the NPE had certified the airplanes. INSURV testing went beyond NPE in determining not only that Vought had complied with all contract specifications but the most effective employment of the aircraft, as well as preparing operating procedures for fleet service. Well before the introduction of the Naval Air Training and Operating Procedures Standardization, or NATOPS, publications, VX-3 was "writing the book" on basic operating characteristics of the Crusader in a fleet environment. The squadron's first F8U-1 was flown into Atlantic City by its Commander Dosé, on 4 December 1956. Arriving immediately afterward Lt. Cdr. Paul Miller brought in the second airplane. Demonstration of carrier launches, approaches, and arrestments began on the USS *Franklin D. Roosevelt* (CVA 42) in April 1957. The timing proved opportune for VX-3's carrier testing of the F8U-1, in that *FDR* had recently completed Ship Characteristics Board (SCB) 110 modernization adding an angled-deck, steam catapults, and a mirror landing system.

That late winter the ship was steaming near Atlantic City toward a set of cold-weather tryouts of the new catapult system. In the trials that followed, no significant discrepancies were noted in ship compatibility for the F8U, even in the landing phase. Yet Dosé's logbook indicates that he "crashed at sea" on approach on 29 March 1957 after a 1.7-hour flight in the F8U-1, having accumulated 13.6 hours in the model.[11] Dosé was rescued. One week later, however, on 6 April, another VX-3 squadron member, Cdr. Ray Boyd, rode his F8U-1 into the sea after his airplane lost power during the catapult stroke (i.e., launch). Boyd was trapped in the airplane as it sank for 80 feet until freed with assistance from a rescue swimmer, but he then became entangled in the parachute harness and drowned, along with the rescue crewman.[12] The

VX-3 F8U-1 refuels from an AJ Savage. (Vought Heritage Foundation)

Carrier suitability trials were expanded with VX-3. Here, a VX-3 F8U-1 is hoisted aboard the USS *Franklin D. Roosevelt* (CVA 42) on 31 March 1957. (NARA)

VX-3 pilots exit their F8U-1s on the *Roosevelt*'s flight deck. (NARA)

Franklin D. Roosevelt, a late-war *Midway*-class ship on which VX-3 did its carrier suitability work, had a flight deck much smaller than Commander Windsor had seen earlier on the *Forrestal*. VX-3's work would prove the more apt demonstration, as in the next decade Crusaders would be confined to *Midway*s and even smaller *Essex*-class decks, as the F-4 Phantom went to *Forrestal*- and later-class carriers.

NOTES

1. George Spangenberg, Interview by Capt. Rosario Rausa, USN (Ret.), September 1989, Oral History Project, National Naval Aviation Museum, accessed at http://aviationarchives.blogspot.com/2018/02/george-spangenberg-oral-history.html.

2. Cdr. T. M. Kastner, USN, "The Navy Preliminary Evaluation: Its Role in the Development of Naval Aircraft," AIAA Conference Paper, American Institute of Aeronautics and Astronautics, 25 March 1968, accessed at https://arc.aiaa.org/doi/abs/10.2514/6.1968-265.

3. Robert W. "Duke" Windsor, Captain, USN (Ret.), Interview by Donald R. Lennon, 6 February 1988, Oral History Project OH0107, East Carolina University, accessed at https://digital.lib.ecu.edu/special/ead/findingaids/oh0107?q=Windsor.

4. Maj. Lynn Helms, "Gator Tales," Crusader Association, accessed June 2024 at https://www.f8crusader.org.

5. Col. John Glenn, USMC (Ret.), with Nick Taylor, *John Glenn: A Memoir* (Bantam Books, 1999), 217.

6. Windsor interview.

7. Spidle, 76

8. Chance Vought Aircraft, "F8U-1P Detail Specification, SD-500-1-1," August 1955, NARA, College Park, MD.

9. Douglas E. Campbell, *Flight, Camera, Action* (Syneca Research, 2014), 401.

10. George F. Rodgers, Cdr., USN (Ret.), "Drafting Board to Mothballs," (Chief of Naval Operations, Washington, DC), *Naval Aviation News* (September 1957), 1.

11. Curt Dosé, Cdr., USN (Ret.), Interview by Ernest Snowden, 10 June 2024.

12. "Raymond A. Boyd, Cdr., USN," U.S. Naval Academy Virtual Memorial Hall, accessed 19 July 2024 at https://usnamemorialhall.org/index.php/RAYMOND_A._BOYD,_CDR,_USN.

HONOR AND ACCLAIM

Commander Windsor stands in his F8U-1 cockpit on 21 August 1956 after setting the speed record that would earn the Thompson Trophy. (U.S. Naval Institute photo archive)

John Konrad in the XF8U-1 on 25 March 1955 had set a new record by reaching supersonic speed on a new type's first flight. The immediate effect was putting naval aviation on par with the Air Force, arriving at a new plateau in performance with a carrier-based fighter design. More accolades were soon to follow.

PROJECT ONE GRAND

In its earliest incarnation, the Thompson Trophy was all about speed and maneuverability. The competition involved flying around a closed ten-mile course, requiring of the pilot tight, high-g turns around 50-foot-high pylons. Awarded annually at the National Air Races, it was an artifact of the "golden age of flight" in the 1930s. When it restarted after being discontinued during World War II, supercharged propeller-powered warbirds briefly held sway until the National Aeronautical Association (NAA), which sanctioned Thompson Trophy records, opened a category for military jets in 1951. For the next five years, Air Force jets took home the Thompson honors.

The arrival of the F8U-1 held out the promise of an upset. Robert Windsor drew the assignment. Windsor was in the right job at the right time, already deeply engaged in testing the F8U's flying qualities; he brought with him a lot of experience. Windsor had flown Wildcats with a composite squadron off an escort carrier during World War II and served on the staff of legendary Adm. Marc Mitscher before the war ended. By the mid-1950s he had served a first tour as a project test pilot at Pax River, had commanded two jet squadrons, from the *Yorktown* and the *Kearsarge*, and was back at NATC as a seasoned senior project test pilot. Windsor was the fourth Navy pilot to reach a thousand hours in jet aircraft.

Cdr. "Duke" Windsor and Mr. Fred Crawford, representing trophy sponsor Thompson Products, pose with the Thompson Trophy. The F8U-1 in the background, flown by Windsor for the record, was a standard production-model Crusader with four Colt cannons installed and a dummy weight equaling that of 16 2.75-inch Mighty Mouse rockets and a full load of 20-mm ammunition. (NNAM)

In 1956 the NAA established a new protocol for timing Thompson Trophy runs, installing two ten-inch telephoto cameras, pointing up, at each end of the course, aligned north-and-south in the Mojave Desert. Beginning with Windsor's F8U run and all Thompson Trophy attempts that followed, the overflight of the airplane triggered a flash of the camera and a recording of the precise time for later analysis by NAA to establish exact speed between north and south camera stations. Supplementing the cameras were theodolite cameras positioned along the course to film the airplanes passing by. Triangulation of the theodolite images served as a backup confirmation of actual speed. Additionally, two barographs, to record altitude, and two cameras in a compartment behind the pilot in the twelfth production Crusader, chosen for the event. Two more barographs and two more cameras, which recorded a duplicate set of flight instruments, were installed in the ammunition bay, and a radar marker beacon was installed in the rocket pack. The aircraft retained its four 20-mm guns—less ammunition—for the record runs. Finally, the undersides of the outer wing panels and the vertical tail were painted in high-visibility orange to help ground observers. Windsor remembered, "I went out to the desert and we did about eight or nine warm-up flights. We cooled the fuel through dry ice so you get more fuel in the airplane."[1] The dry-ice cooling reduced the volume of the jet fuel enough to permit about 300 more pounds to be pumped into the airplane's tanks. The Crusader was towed to the runway from its hangar at Marine Corps Auxiliary Air Station Mojave, to preserve fuel that would otherwise be consumed in a powered taxi to the runway.

At 6:50 a.m., Windsor was airborne, headed to the southern course marker. At 32,000 feet, he moved the throttle past the detent into afterburner, almost immediately passing 1.0 Mach. Passing the south marker, ninety miles from Mojave, he turned back north for the first recorded leg, reaching 40,000 feet. He hit the north marker at 1,018.5 miles per hour. At that speed the turn back toward the south marker sent him eighty-five miles away from the course before Windsor recovered a heading to the south marker. On his second run he was recorded at 1,012.3 miles per hour, for an average speed of 1,015.4 miles per hour.[2]

Windsor later recalled, "The name of the project [i.e., within the Navy] was Project One Grand because we wanted to hit one thousand miles an hour and be the first ones to do it. We did, without any strain. We could have gone faster if they had allowed us to. The Secretary of Defense was [Charles E.] Wilson at that time and he said, 'I don't want you to go over a thousand miles an hour.' He didn't want the Russians to know what a superb airplane it was. I had it up over eleven hundred miles an hour. That airplane could really move out."[3]

THE COLLIER TROPHY

In the history of American aeronautics, the Collier Trophy stands as the foremost recognition of design excellence. Awarded annually, it is revered in much the same manner as the Oscar in the realm of motion picture arts and sciences. It has been bestowed on Orville Wright, Glenn Curtiss, Glenn Martin, Donald Douglas, Chuck Yeager, Ed Heinemann, Kelly Johnson, and Gen. "Hap" Arnold, names in the pantheon of historic aviators and engineers. Donated in 1911 by Robert Collier, an early aviation enthusiast and close friend of Orville Wright, the prize is awarded each year for "the greatest achievement in America with respect to improving performance, efficiency and safety of air vehicles, the value of which has been thoroughly demonstrated by actual use during the preceding year."[4]

Individual Collier Trophy replicas of the large original trophy held at the National Air and Space Museum are presented to Vice Adm. James Russell, chief of the Bureau of Aeronautics, and Charles McCarthy, chairman of the board of Vought Aircraft Company. Officiating, at right, is Thomas Lanphier, president of the National Aeronautics Association. (*Crusader Fighter Report*)

Only twice in the forty-five years before the Crusader won it had the Collier been awarded to a fighter aircraft, and only one of those two awards had gone to another Navy fighter aircraft. The 1956 recipients of the Collier Trophy were Charles McCarthy, chairman, on behalf of Chance Vought Aircraft Company, and Vice Adm. James Russell, chief of the Bureau of Aeronautics for the U.S. Navy, for superior achievement in "conception, design, and development of the F8U Crusader, a carrier-based fighter which is the first operational aircraft capable of speeds exceeding one thousand miles an hour." Speed was of surpassing importance in the competitive criteria, yet speed was not the whole story. The Collier Award committee took into consideration that here was a design that permitted a pilot in one instance to obtain supersonic speed and then, with the movement of a single lever, reconfigure the aircraft for landing on a Navy flight deck. The way in which the wing flaps and leading-edge droops were linked to the selected incidence angle of the wing so that they automatically lowered when the wing was raised, or raised when the wing was brought back down; the use of an intermediate cruise droop to give the airplane manageable subsonic maneuverability with a thin-wing design at high altitude and low Q—both evidenced the brilliance of the Vought design and value of the Navy partnership that nudged Vought on.

Although unnamed in the official Collier correspondence, many people at Vought shared in the accomplishment. That group at the very least included Frank Detweiler, president; Harold Sallada, executive assistant to Detweiler and former head of BuAer when on active duty; Ray Blalock, engineering vice president; Russ Clark, chief engineer; Lyman Josephs, F8U project engineer; and, certainly, John Konrad, chief test pilot. In the panel that selected this prestigious joint award of the 1956 Collier were empaneled twenty-seven prominent figures in U.S. aviation, among them Tom Lanphier, who shared credit for downing Adm. Isoroku's Yamamoto aircraft during the war, and Jackie Cochran, winner of the Bendix Trophy and the first woman to reach 1.0 Mach.

PROJECT BULLET

Major Glenn left active flight testing of the F8U in late fall of 1956 but remained attached to the airplane as a BuAer project officer in the VF Fighter Design Branch. A significant part of his responsibility at BuAer was sorting through the increasing flow of F8U engineering change proposals so as to prioritize the most critical and immediate for funding. One of the proposed changes was to correct an afterburner reliability issue. He became intrigued by the possibility of conclusively demonstrating engine reliability while at the same time resetting the transcontinental speed record, another distinction then held by the Air Force. At some point between conceiving such a flight and getting approval, it occurred to him that the Crusader actually flew faster than the muzzle velocity of a .45-caliber bullet. He had struck on the name for the demonstration: Project Bullet. To persuade the more reticent senior officers in BuAer, he pitched the demonstration as the ideal capstone for the testing program: a sustained maximum speed, maximum altitude, max-Mach-number long-distance flight. The senior officers finally gave in, but they wanted the assurance of backups in the event that a single airplane or pilot—Glenn would be the primary—failed to complete the project flight. A second Crusader was duly assigned, as well as a second pilot: Lt. Cdr. Charles Demmler was detached from his project test pilot duties at Patuxent River to join the planning for the demonstration.

The record setting protocol was again—as with Cdr. Windsor's flight—in the purview of the NAA, acting as the American representative to the final aviation records-sanctioning body, the Fédération Aéronautique Internationale in Paris. The team was allowed two weeks to put together a complicated attempt on the record, which necessitated more seniority to push preparations along. Rear Adm. T. B. Clark, commanding the Naval Air Test Center, was installed as the team leader, assisted by Cdr. Jess Barker, NATC Service Test Division chief, managing a combined team of military and Vought personnel.

The plan required a Crusader to be refueled three times enroute during a 2,445-mile flight. The Air Force, which had the only jet tankers, rebuffed Glenn's invitation to collaborate in challenging the record they currently held. Navy twin-prop AJ Savage tankers sufficed but complicated the planning, because they could maintain only 300 miles per hour at 25,000 feet. One practice flight with an AJ ended in near-tragedy. With Glenn plugged into its fuel drogue, the tanker's reciprocating engines began smoking. The three AJ crew members had to bail out just before the airplane plowed into the open prairie north of Dallas. All survived, and Glenn had made an emergency breakaway, decelerating his F8U to pull his fuel probe away from the AJ's drogue, but the episode reminded everyone of the risks to life and reputation that were involved.

After many practice refuelings, three sites were selected at which to stage the AJs: Albuquerque, New Mexico; Olathe, Kansas; and Columbus, Ohio. Detailed planning for waypoints and rendezvous procedures went into high gear. Vought assumed the major responsibility for flight profile planning and technical assistance. The Continental Air Defense Command, predecessor of today's North American Air Defense Command, was brought in to assure radar coverage for the entire flight. Aerologists were stationed at both ends of the

In one of a series of practice refuelings, John Glenn waits his turn as wingman Demmler plugs behind a VAH-11 AJ1. (Vought Heritage Foundation)

Lt. Cdr. Charles Demmler flew as Major Glenn's wingman for Project Bullet in an F8U-1; however, damage to his aircraft during aerial refueling prevented Demmler from completing the cross-country flight. (Vought Heritage Foundation)

Glenn props himself on the canopy rail of the F8U-1P that he flew from NAS Los Alamitos, California, to NAS Floyd Bennett Field, New York, to set a cross-country speed record. (Vought Heritage Foundation)

Glenn and Demmler line up for takeoff from Los Alamitos before their cross-country speed run to Floyd Bennett Field. Glenn completed the flight, clocking an average speed of 725.55 miles per hour. (NARA)

Glenn prior to his cross-country record-setting attempt. (Vought Heritage Foundation)

Capt. Robert Dosé and wingman Lt. Cdr. Paul Miller take position on the USS *Bon Homme Richard's* bow catapults before launching on their cross-country flight from Pacific waters to the USS *Saratoga* (CV 60), steaming off Florida. (NARA)

route for hour-by-hour weather forecasting, supported by weather reporting from a pathfinder A3D Skywarrior launched one hour ahead of the flight. Because NAA rules required that takeoff and landing airports be within a sixty-kilometer radius of stated origination and arrival points, Los Angeles International Airport (LAX) and Floyd Bennett Field in New York City were chosen for takeoff and landing, respectively. Just hours before things were set to go, LAX officials balked at afterburner takeoffs. All the fuel, starters, and special equipment had to be trucked to an alternate takeoff runway within the required sixty kilometers. Glenn finally got under way at 6:04 a.m. local time on 16 July 1957 from Naval Air Station Los Alamitos. Passing through a low overcast, he reached 30,000 feet and accelerated. As the plane lightened from the burning of fuel he picked up speed to 1.48 Mach, climbing to 51,000 feet. Demmler took off 30 minutes later.

The first tanker rendezvous was over Grants, New Mexico. Glenn had to slow considerably to match the AJ's speed, which took more than forty miles. When he "made the plug" the tanker pilot joked, "Check under the hood?" To which Glenn responded, "Don't bother. I'm in sort of a hurry this morning."[5] The second refueling, over Emporia, Kansas, went smoothly for Glenn, but Demmler hit the drogue too hard and was unable to refuel. He left the mission at that point, landing safely. The third rendezvous did not go as planned for Glenn, now on his own in the pursuit of the record. In the haze at 25,000 feet, Glenn was unable to spot the tanker and spent precious minutes "burning down" an already depleted set of fuel tanks looking for it. The orbiting AJ spotted Glenn and guided him to the rendezvous but could only partially replenish the F8U's tanks before he had to break away to stay on schedule.

Sonic booms trailed Glenn across the country. Near his hometown in Ohio, ceilings collapsed and windows broke. A neighbor hurried to Glenn's residence exclaiming to his mother, "Mrs. Glenn, Johnny dropped a bomb, Johnny dropped a bomb."[6] Glenn passed the tower at Floyd Bennett Field with only three hundred pounds of fuel remaining, clocked at 3 hours, 23 minutes, and 8.4 seconds. He had broken the record by twenty-one minutes. Twenty-months later, when accepted into the first NASA astronaut class, he was already a nationally known personality.

RAPID CAPABILITY DEMONSTRATION

Five weeks before Major Glenn's Project Bullet, a less official but no less important demonstration involving the F8U-1 was conducted by VX-3. On 6 June 1957, President Dwight Eisenhower boarded the USS *Saratoga* (CVA 60) in Naval Station Mayport, Florida, for two days of underway aerial demonstrations by the embarked air group. The president and cabinet members were escorted aboard by Secretary of the Navy Thomas Gates, CNO Adm. Arleigh Burke, and Commander-in-Chief Atlantic Fleet, Adm. Jerauld Wright. In late May, just a week prior to the president's visit, Bob Dosé, commanding VX-3, had received a call from the CNO's staff asking if a demonstration could be arranged that underscored naval aviation's ability to shift carrier planes from ocean to ocean without intermediate landings ashore. This was not to be accorded "project" status so as not to distract from Project Bullet, then in the final planning stage. Rather, it would be treated as reflecting an everyday fleet capability that also highlighted the range and speed performance of the Navy's newest jet fighter.

Dosé and his VX-3 wingman, Lt. Cdr. Paul Miller, traveled to the Vought factory near Dallas from Atlantic City to pick up two F8U-1's configured for in-flight

Pilots of Crusaders and A3D Skywarriors from a carrier on the West Coast and another across the nation on the East Coast meet with President Dwight D. Eisenhower after completion of the flight aboard the *Saratoga*. Foreground (*left to right*): Captain Dosé, wingman Lieutenant Commander Miller, VX-3 F8U-1 project officer, President Eisenhower, A3D pilots Lt. Cdr. John Miller and Lt. Cdr. C. C. McBratnie. (NHHC)

refueling and flew them to the West Coast. At NAS Alameda, California, the airplanes were hoisted aboard the USS *Bon Homme Richard* (CVA 31), which was to transit to waters off San Diego. Meanwhile, as part of the demonstration, two Douglas A3D Skywarriors of VAH-9 launched from the *Bon Homme Richard* and proceeded eastward without any aerial refueling planned on their way.

The two F8U-1s launched from the *Bon Homme Richard* and climbed in afterburner to 43,000 feet. Coming out of burner, they headed toward a planned rendezvous near Dallas with AJ2 tankers. Thirteen minutes prior to descending to refuel, they conducted a preplanned afterburner light-off to accelerate to 1.7 Mach. Rendezvous completed and fully refueled, they lighted afterburners again for the climb back to 43,000 feet, coming out of burner once reaching altitude. Another preplanned afterburner light-off occurred over Alabama, seventeen minutes from their descent toward *Saratoga*, steaming in the Atlantic. The airplane was straining at the bit to exceed 1.7 Mach, so Dosé led the flight into a shallow climb to hold that speed.

Nearing Jacksonville, about ten miles inland from Mayport, Dosé visually sighted *Saratoga* about fifty miles offshore surrounded by her escorts. Now at 50,000 feet, the two VX-3 pilots went to idle power and held their throttles there through their descent, dodging towering thunder clouds most of the way down. Still at idle, the two passed up the carrier's port side at 100 feet and close to 1.0 Mach. Now rapidly losing speed but still not bringing their throttles out of idle position, the two traveled upwind braking hard to bleed off excess speed. When sufficiently slowed on the downwind leg, Dosé and his wingman—now "in trail" in the ship's landing pattern—raised their wings and dropped their gear. Throttles were still at idle at the 180-degree position relative to the ship, or dead astern, as each started his turn into the approach. Coming through the "ninety-degree position," halfway through his turn, Dosé realized he hadn't halted the drop in airspeed quickly enough and now added power just as he crossed the ramp, in a flat approach to a "three-wire," his tailhook catching the middle of five arresting-gear cables—perfect.[7] (The aftmost portion of the carrier flight deck extends somewhat beyond the ship's transom, or stern, and is sloped noticeably downward; its curved extremity is the "round down," or "ramp.")

The two pilots taxied up to the island structure and climbed out of their aircraft, to be met by members of the press. They had launched from a carrier in the Pacific and recovered on a carrier in the Atlantic without landing in between, in an unofficial record time of three hours and twenty-eight minutes. President Eisenhower was brought from an observation post high in the island on the flag bridge down to the flight deck to congratulate them and the two A3D pilots, who had landed shortly before the F8U-1s. Dosé was to remember President Eisenhower as "a very impressive gentleman who was very interested in all the details of our flight."[8]

NAVY CERTIFICATE OF MERIT

In a first for an aircraft manufacturer, Secretary Gates presented to the Chance Vought Aircraft Company the Navy Department Certificate of Merit. This honor, as described by official instruction, befitted only associations or corporations that had rendered outstanding service to the Department of the Navy. Not limited to any individual's contribution, it recognized the entire company's achievement in the design and development of the F8U Crusader. The nomination, forwarded for the secretary's signature by the chief of the Bureau of Aeronautics, Rear Adm. James Russell, singled out the company's performance against contract specifications and its ability to deliver on promises made as significantly beneficial to the accomplishment of the overall mission of the Navy and Marine Corps.

NOTES

1. Windsor interview.

2. William A. Kinsley, Commander, USN, "F8U Wins Thompson Trophy," (Chief of Naval Operations, Washington, DC), *Naval Aviation News* (October 1956), https://www.history.navy.mil/research/histories/, 1–13.

3. Kinsley.

4. National Aeronautics Association, "The Collier Trophy," accessed 19 July 2024 at https://naa.aero/awards/awards-trophies/collier-trophy/.

5. Glenn, *Memoir*, 225.

6. Glenn.

7. Dosé interview.

8. William A. Kinsley, Commander, USN, "Navy Planes Span Nation," (Chief of Naval Operations, Washington, DC), *Naval Aviation News*, (August 1957), https://www.history.navy.mil/research/histories/, 8.

NAVAL AVIATION ENTERS THE SUPERSONIC AGE

VF-32 "Swordsmen" F8U-1E comes aboard the *Saratoga* just two years after the Crusader was first introduced to a fleet squadron, VF-32. (Lawson Coll., Buehler Naval Aviation Library, NNAM)

(inset) VF-32's squadron insignia, the "Swordsmen," evokes its connection with its new Crusader mounts. (NHHC)

Operational testing with VX-3 had barely begun when early in 1957 the first Crusaders began arriving on the ramp at Cecil Field in Florida, intended for a fleet squadron, Fighter Squadron 32. The "Swordsmen" of VF-32 were the first to receive the new F8U-1. On the West Coast, VF(AW)-3 at Moffett Field was next in line. VF(AW)-3 (the *AW* denoting all-weather capability) was the transition/refresher-training squadron for aviators returning to the fleet to F4D or F3H squadrons. The squadron already functioned something like the Fleet Replacement Squadron, or FRS, that would appear officially later and would indeed be the blueprint for the Readiness Air Group concept. With tongue somewhat in cheek, the squadron now brandished the nickname "School of Supersonic Knowledge" to acknowledge the arrival of the F8U.[1]

FLEET INTRODUCTION

These two squadrons were incorporated into the F8U Fleet Introduction Plan, or FIP, an accelerated eight-week test program to learn the airplane's capabilities. Aviators and maintainers were assessed on their ability to "own" (take custody of and responsibility for), operate, and maintain the airplane, with a focus on training pilots in the F8U to act as an initial instructor cadre when returning to their home bases.

Fighter Squadron 32 sent eleven pilots and ground officers with eighty enlisted maintainers to Patuxent River, where they were joined by six pilots and fifty maintainers from VF(AW)-3. Small numbers of pilots from VX-3 joined the group, hosted by NATC's Service Test Branch, headed by Capt. Don Gay. Once on board, they essentially merged into a combined unit for training under VF(AW)-3's skipper, Cdr. Reid Stone, and VF-32's, Cdr. George Buhrer, taking the role of operations officer.

Vought mechanics mentored the enlisted maintainers, who gradually took over all the hangar and flight-line maintenance under the watchful eye of the contractor reps. The maintainers had all been to Vought's ground school in aircraft systems at Grand Prairie or at a minimum had spent time in the mobile F8U maintenance trainer at Cecil Field. Before climbing into cockpits, pilots spent several days in the classroom intently absorbing briefings from NATC test pilots on spin-recovery techniques and, more generally, the up-and-away performance of the Crusader. These classroom sessions for pilots were preceded by several weeks with Vought's engineers and production test pilots in Grand Prairie going over aircraft systems and cockpit procedures. Before their cockpit checkouts, all pilots had to endure the low-pressure oxygen chamber to adapt themselves to a new oxygen system they would find in the Crusader.

When VF-32 and VF(AW)-3 members finished their transition training, they returned to their respective bases on East and West Coasts, some of them flying Crusaders there as transition training assets for squadrons designated to get the aircraft. "The plane was mocked up only a little over three years before it reached the FIP phase. Only 21 months intervened between the first flight on 25 March 1955 and FIP."[2] Now, in just another twelve months, VF-32 joined Carrier Air Group 3 (CVG-3) in the USS *Saratoga*, in December 1957, departing for the Mediterranean two months later. VF-32 thus became the first squadron to take the Crusader on a regular carrier deployment—and it would be an eventful cruise.

F8U-2 of VF-32 on elevator of the *Saratoga* in 1959. (ALAMY)

In July 1958 14,000 Marines and Army troops were put ashore in Lebanon, to bolster a friendly Lebanese government against incursions by pro-Soviet Syrian and Egyptian forces. The *Saratoga* was one of three carriers assigned to support them. VF-32 was to make an aerial show of force and fly combat air patrols over the U.S. personnel. As part of the show of strength, shortly after the troops were sent in VF-32 F8Us joined an eleven-plane formation in a sweep over Lebanon and down the Jordan River to Jordan. In all, the squadron flew 730 combat air patrol missions in direct support of the ground deployment over three months. To keep the squadron at full strength, four replacement aircraft were delivered midcruise by pilots from VX-3. Originating at NAS Oceana, they went by way of Brunswick, Maine; Argentia, Newfoundland; and the Azores to Port Lyautey, Morocco. For the longest leg, the 1,525 miles from Oceana to the Azores, the Crusaders were topped off enroute by AJ aerial tankers. At Port Lyautey four VF-32 squadron members—Lt. Cdr. John Stetson, Lt. Howard Rutledge, Lt. "Dog" Davison, and Lt. (jg) Charles Lusk—picked up the Crusaders and flew them the last 1,100 miles to the *Saratoga*. Before the cruise, all VF-32 pilots entered the "One Grand Club," going 1,000 mph in their F8Us. During the cruise, every VF-32 pilot became a "Crusader Centurion," by making at least 100 arrested landings.

F8U-2s of the Fighting Shamrocks of VMF-333 launch from the USS *Forrestal*. (Buehler Naval Aviation Library, NNAM)

When the contingency subsided, USS *Saratoga* was replaced on station by the USS *Forrestal*, which brought with her the first Marine squadron to have transitioned to the F8U, VMF-333. The "Fighting Shamrocks" maintained watch over the de-escalating crisis in Lebanon, returning to Beaufort, South Carolina, to become in 1960 the first Marine squadron to exchange its F8U-1s for F8U-2s (as described later in this chapter).

Meanwhile, the "Grand Slammers" of VF-154 became the first West Coast fleet squadron to receive F8U-1s. It was cause for a name change, to the "Black Knights," a reference to their Crusader mounts. VF-154's initial cadre of transition pilots and maintainers were mentored at Moffett Field by VF(AW)-3's trained Crusader operators. VF-154 pilot Lt. (jg) Bob Miottel later recalled that Lt. Col. John Glenn, late of Project Bullet fame and then with BuAer's Fighter Design Branch, accompanied the squadron aboard the USS *Hancock* to impart Crusader knowledge prior to its first Carrier-Qualification period with the airplane.

REPLACEMENT AIR GROUPS

F8U Crusaders arrived in Navy fleet squadrons nearly simultaneously with other advanced jet fighter aircraft of the era: the F4D, F3H, and F11F. All the new jet squadrons, F-8 squadrons among them, experienced upticks in mishap rates. This was an inevitable outcome of introducing so many new, advanced aircraft without a standardized training syllabus in place across naval aviation for each type and model aircraft.

For VF-154 the mishap numbers were sobering. Yet VF-154's experience was not outside the norm for squadrons transitioning to the F8U or radically different from 1950s fighter transition statistics generally. In 1957, the year of the squadron's transition from the FJ Fury to the F8U, it lost fourteen aircraft and eight pilots, five of those killed and three obliged by their injuries to leave active flying. With unprecedented power and

(above) Lt. (jg) Robert Miottel of VF-154 became the first West Coast fleet Crusader pilot to carrier-qualify in the Crusader. Miottel also became one of the first on that coast with multiple barrier engagements. Flight-deck personnel surround Miottel's second barricade episode in three months. (Robert Miottel)

Miottel takes a closer look at the damage to the tail of his Crusader resulting from contact with the barricade netting. Miottel is sporting a customized but officially approved squadron ballcap. (Buehler Naval Aviation Library, NNAM)

ONE FIVE FOUR

Discarding its previous squadron insignia showing a flaming black panther on a yellow background, VF-154, the "Black Knights," adopted a new insignia more befitting its new Crusader. Cartoonist Milt Caniff finalized the artwork. (Robert Miottel) performance came a corresponding rise in accident rates; Crusaders were being flown to and sometimes beyond the limit of their airworthiness. Pilot error accounted for most of the mishap rate, but materiel failure contributed too. Breakage of aileron linkage, landing strut collapse, and tailhook-shank separation were typical causes. Records indicate that by the year of the Crusader's retirement from active fleet service 1,106 F-8s out of a total production number of 1,261 aircraft had been involved in accidents—88 percent, many of them left unsalvageable. By far, the first year of introduction, 1957, yielded the highest accident rate, 244 mishaps per 100,000 flight hours.[3]

The aircraft carrier landing pattern was the most difficult challenge. Night or foul weather surely heightened every experience "in the groove." While more senior squadron pilots with many hours "flying the ball" (i.e., landing on carriers, with the aid of the Optical Landing System, or OLS) managed reasonably consistent "boarding" rates, junior pilots, either fresh from the training command or in transition from another aircraft had their hands full. That was never more apparent than when VF-154 went to sea aboard USS *Hancock* in late 1957 for its first "Carrier Qualification" period. Bob Miottel had already "CQ'ed" (carrier qualified) in the FJ Fury, but knew that he was now starting over, on a different learning curve. He later recalled losing a fellow pilot on approach to *Hancock* when his port landing gear was lost in a "ramp strike" (collision with the ship's stern after a too-low approach) and subsequently ejecting "out of the envelope" (i.e., in conditions for which the ejection system was not designed). Miottel's own approach was complicated by a tailhook that had slewed out of position and stuck that way. He was too far from shore to fly to the field, so he was directed to "take the barricade"—the heavy safety net—without attempting to hook the arresting wires. The force of hitting the barricade off-center collapsed Miottel's left landing-gear strut, sending his airplane over the side into the water, where it was dragged by the barricade strapping. Miottel extracted himself and swam away to be picked up by the safety helicopter. Three months later another broken tailhook gave Miottel another barricade landing from which he was able to walk away.[4]

The Fleet Introduction Program for the Crusader, while successful to a degree in transitioning pilots to jets of a new type, model, or series, could not alone correct the disturbing mishap trend. Dedicated, consistent aviation-community-wide training in all aspects of fleet operation was addressed head-on in March 1958 when "the CNO approved permanent

First F8U to arrive at Moffett Field for the second West Coast fleet squadron transitioning to the Crusader, VF-211. Pictured with the F8U-1 in 1957 are (*left to right*): Lieutenants Jim Stockdale and Paul Pugh, with Lt. Cdr. "Red Dog" Davis, squadron CO. (Buehler Naval Aviation Library, NNAM)

Readiness Air Groups on each coast with responsibility for indoctrination of key technicians, tactical training of aircrew, and implementing special programs required for the introduction of new combat aircraft models."[5]

The Readiness Air Group concept (RCVG) and its attendant Type/Model Fleet Replacement Squadrons (FRSs) were stood up, RCVG-4 on the East Coast and RCVG-12 on the West. Under the respective "RAGs," as the RCVGs were and still are often known, FRS VF-174 stood up at Cecil Field to standardize Crusader training for pilots reporting to East Coast squadrons, and FRS VF-124—or "Crusader College," first at NAS Moffett, then at NAS Miramar—did the same for West Coast squadrons.

F8U-1s of VF-62, normally embarked in the USS *Shangri-La* (CVA-38), line up on the USS *Enterprise* (CVN 65) for carrier qualification. VF-62 in 1960 became the fifth East Coast squadron to transition to the Crusader. (Lawson Coll., Buehler Naval Aviation Library, NNAM)

Designed for students fresh from the training command (where they had earned the wing devices marking them as naval aviators) and also experienced aviators who had been absent from the cockpit on shore duty, the course of instruction in these two squadrons began with twenty hours of instrument-refresher flying in the Grumman F9F-8T two-seat Cougar, followed by a flight check. This training also familiarized the Replacement Pilots (RPs) with "area course rules" (regulations for certain types of airspace and geographical areas, applicable to all U.S. aviators) and federal approach and departure procedures. The F8U RP then progressed to Crusader-specific training, beginning with two weeks of systems familiarization in ground school and procedures training in flight simulators. Advancing to airborne instruction in the F8U, the RP was expected to demonstrate proficiency in basic "air work" and touch-and-go landings in six flights in the Crusader, followed closely throughout by an instructor in a second F8U.

Mastery of the airplane demonstrated, the RP moved into the tactics phase of night flying and weapons familiarization, concluding in day and night carrier qualifications. In 18 weeks, the RP typically logged 110 hours in the airplane, comprising 20 hours of instrument refresher and 19 hours of tactics in preparation for F8U squadron assignment.

Crusader pilots benefited immeasurably from this sort of intermediate mentoring when it was time to integrate into a Crusader squadron's operating tempo. A decade later, the statistics showed marked improvement: the highest average monthly accident rate for August from 1969 through 1974 was 61.5 mishaps per 100,000 flight hours. Still, the F-4 Phantom's August mishap average in that same 5-year span was 26.8 per 100,000 flight hours, less than half the Crusader's.[6]

Student Replacement Pilot Lt. (jg) Steve Marinshaw's second flight under instruction was 30 minutes of basic air work in an operating area off San Diego, followed by 30 minutes in the pattern at Miramar until low fuel indicated it was time to land. His second flight was intended to achieve a supersonic dash of 1,000 miles per hour, but cloud layers prohibited a climb to altitude for his supersonic run; students with less than 10 hours in the plane were limited to Visual Flight Rules. His instructor on that flight, in a second aircraft, decided to do some tail-chasing between cloud layers at 2,000 feet and 5,000 feet for confidence-building in strenuous maneuvering. Marinshaw was to remember the next events this way:

> At first his [the instructor's] turns were moderate and holding position was easy. I think one of the tricks the instructors sometimes performed was to gradually increase the turning g's until the student pilot could not remain inside his turn [turn as sharply]. Then he would reverse quickly and fly into position on the student's tail, demonstrating his superiority in air combat maneuvering. I sensed that he was leading into that, but I was confident that anything his airplane could do, mine could do the same. When he increased his turning to high g's, I pulled harder, determined to stay on his tail. I don't know how hard I pulled, but my Crusader swapped ends. Then the airplane started tumbling and I remember bouncing around in the cockpit. My instructor was yelling on the radio, "Let go of the controls, let go of the controls." I did and the nose dropped, and the plane stopped whatever it was doing. I had very little airspeed, so I gently pulled the stick back holding optimum angle-of-attack while accelerating nose-down to recover. I entered the lower cloud deck while leveling off and then climbed back into the clear. My instructor saw me emerge from the undercast and joined me, took the lead, and radioed, "Let's go home." That was it for flight number two. During the debrief, the instructor said, "I was watching you in my mirror and looking down your intake. The next second I was looking up your tailpipe." I learned firsthand how to recover from uncontrolled flight on my second time in the Crusader.[7]

The Crusader had a generous stall-warning margin with adequate cues before departing from normal flight if a pilot knew what to look for. However, distinguishing a post-stall gyration from a fully developed spin could be difficult for the new pilot subjected to wildly disorienting excursions in yaw and pitch. As explained by Richard Linnekin, a contemporary naval aviator and later memoirist, a true poststall gyration could be preceded by an end-over-end tumble much like that experienced by Marinshaw. The recommended response, as called by his instructor, was to neutralize the controls and wait. A true spin in the Crusader, regardless of the violence of the gyrations, could be recognized by continuous turn in the same direction, and more typically, by very high angle of attack on the AoA gauge. Because of some unique features embodied in the Crusader's design, spin recovery was less conventional than in other aircraft. Once the spin was recognized, the pilot would, with a motion of the thumb on a throttle-mounted switch,

> lower the wing leading-edge droop to the landing position to increase the wing's camber, making it better able to "fly" at increased angle of attack. Then if spinning to the left, move the stick all the way back and as far into the left-hand corner as it will go, moving the stabilator down to stream in the relative wind. Moving the right aileron down to create a speed brake effect on the outside wing, tended to then yaw the airplane to the right against the spin. Once the spin movement stopped, the stick position was neutralized to wait for airspeed to build.[8]

SHADOWED BY LANDING MISHAPS

Despite the definite results that FRS training was beginning to yield by 1961, another post-RAG incident gives insight to the unique challenge of carrier landings in the Crusader. Lt. (jg) John "Terry" Kryway of the VF-11 "Red Rippers" was the unfortunate "nugget" (new naval aviator) captured in a widely published series of still photos of a mishap-in-progress. The sequence showed his landing attempt on the *Franklin D. Roosevelt* on 21 October 1961. Lt. Jim Roberts, a former VF-11 pilot, put it this way: "It could have happened to *any* of us flying the *Crusader* aboard the *Roosevelt* that day. Terry was a super outstanding pilot. He was a member of the 'Red Rippers' flight demo team."[9]

Rough seas were heaving the flight deck about when in the last seconds of Kryway's approach, the deck dipped on the backside of a swell. The plane hit hard on the starboard landing gear and the wheel violently bounced up into its well, rupturing the main fuel line and releasing a suspended cloud of fuel. Although the tailhook had snagged an arresting wire, the resistance of the main landing gear stub scraping the flight deck skewed the nose to the side, putting an asymmetrical load on the tailhook and ripping it out of its socket. Dragging on the flight deck, the magnesium in the strut flamed instantly and set fire to the misting fuel. With a landing speed of about 135 knots, "Kryway had about three seconds to see the fire, realize he had flamed out, let go of the controls, reach for the face curtain and pull it the full eighteen inches required to initiate the ejection sequence"[10]

One frame from a sequence of photos that captured the ramp strike and ejection of Lt. (jg) John "Terry" Kryway of VF-11. (Lawson Coll., Buehler Naval Aviation Library, NNAM)

Squadron commander Edward H. Loftin, in his endorsement of the accident report, echoed Lieutenant Roberts' sentiment but ascribed the mishap to Kryway's singular fixation on getting his F-8 aboard. Loftin wrote that Kryway "is one of the best pilots in the squadron. He is technically competent in all phases of fighter type flying. He is an alert, aggressive pilot with exceptionally fast reflexes. Since carrier quals in December 1960, he has made sixteen landings marked either 'Fair' or 'OK' passes with no bolters [go-arounds having missed all arresting wires] or technique wave-offs. As the unbroken string of successful landings is enhanced so does the anxiety to preserve this record settle onto the subconscious mind. As in this case, although the pilot does not consciously remember reducing power at the ramp, the power was in fact reduced. The subconscious mind, in my opinion[,] was responsible for allowing the pilot to go for the deck which was dropping out from under him [i.e., to force the aircraft to land]. The pilot must be conditioned to know that once he finds himself at the ramp, no correction can be made for a high ball [OLS indication that the aircraft is too high] or line up. The only correction for a low ball is power."[11]

The challenge with the Crusader in-close on approach, immediately before setting down, never diminished. Unfortunately, by the time a low ball was recognized, an increase-power call from the landing signal officer (LSO) on the flight deck in sight of the aircraft, came too late for the engine to respond. In September 1965, a section of F-8Es from VF-194 were returning from a night "barrier combat air patrol," a protective screen for the carrier against threatening enemy aircraft. Having marshaled the section over the carrier, the USS *Bon Bomme Richard*, at his assigned approach time the leader "pushed" over to start an instrument approach to where he could see the ball on final approach. The formation leader landed successfully. Lt. (jg) Denis Duffy, his wingman, started down only minutes after his leader. Descending, Duffy reported altitude changes to the ship's Carrier Air Traffic Control Center (CATCC), using the call sign for the *Bon Homme Richard*, "Rocket," and his own, "Red Flash 212." As he continuing inbound at four thousand feet and 225 knots indicated airspeed, events unfolded something like this:

CATCC: "Red Flash two-one-two, dirty up [extend flaps and landing gear]. Left two degrees."
RF212: "Two-one-two."
CATCC: "Red Flash two-one-two, final control—approaching glide slope, begin descent."

RF212: "Two-one-two."
CATCC: "Two-one-two, on glide slope slightly left of course."
CATCC: "Slightly below glide slope. Continue zero niner two."
CATCC: "No need for further transmissions. Right two degrees."
CATCC: "Slightly above glide slope, on course. Three quarters of a mile, call the ball [report when you see it]."
RF212: "Red Flash two-one-two, Crusader ball, two point seven, manual."
LSO: "Roger ball."
LSO: "You're drifting right, come left for lineup."
LSO: "You're low, don't settle."
LSO: "*Power!*"
LSO: "*Power!*"
LSO: "*Wave off! Wave off!*" [attempt with emergency thrust to get into the air again].

Duffy's nose dropped almost imperceptibly. In a split second, he was beset by factors largely beyond his control. His main landing-gear mounts collided with the ship below the round down and sheared off in a shower of sparks. Hydraulic fluid misting from the stub of his left main gear caught fire, sending a plume of roiling orange and black flame trailing behind the aircraft in a scene reminiscent of Kryway's arrestment four years before. Duffy instinctively jammed the throttle to full power, got into the air again, and with great presence of mind and coolness under extreme pressure, maintained a near-constant attitude without over-rotating and losing control in a stall, thereby allowing his airspeed to build up. But he was rapidly losing flight control authority as hydraulic fluid bled from the sheared-off main mounts. When his aircraft cleared the ship the air boss [the ship's air officer, managing flight operations from high in the island] called for ejection, but Duffy's face curtain was already down over his mask and his seat was powering up and out of the cockpit.

Lieutenant (junior grade) Duffy was an exceptionally promising new aviator—the best pilot among the first-tour nuggets in VF-194. A Crusader nugget but hardly a novice, he had already logged 600 hours in F-8s in this squadron and in the FRS, VF-124, with thrity-fiv traps at night. Like other nuggets, he had been screened throughout flight training for skills deemed essential for assignment to the F-8: superb airmanship, confident deportment, and an innate aggressiveness in the air. Yet . . .

Ramp strikes in the F-8 community were not commonplace; neither were they rare. Accident records indicate that Air Wings 5, 16, 19, and 21 all experienced at least two Crusader ramp strikes during their 1965 deployments to Southeast Asia.[12] With its characteristic raised wing and wing-edge droop, the Crusader was at that point about ten knots above stall speed—not much margin. And things could deteriorate quickly. If airspeed lowered even imperceptibly, drag increased and the aircraft began to settle. As the "settle" steepened, the pilot gently raised the nose and started tweaking the throttle. If drag increased and altitude was lost, the situation could become irretrievable. Before realizing it, the pilot would find himself on the wrong side of the power curve, losing altitude faster than he could compensate for the loss with added power. Crusader pilots could experience this excursion from an acceptable approach profile to out-of-control in split seconds. A former skipper of F-8 squadron VF-111 remembered that there was a window of only a few knots airspeed in which a pilot had to operate when on approach before things quickly got out of hand.[13] Night landings, without visual cues, were worse. And on the older converted *Essex*-class carriers the "window" the F-8 pilot had to fly through to snatch the third of only four cross-deck wires (newer ships had five) gave him no more than ten feet of clearance between the tailhook and the ramp—if he flew an on-speed, centered ball approach all the way to touchdown. Landing accidents in the F8U community tended to drive an uncomfortable mishap rate well beyond that seen during the initial introduction of the airplane.

Flying the F8U in the carrier landing environment demanded well-practiced technique, and even so the very narrow tolerances in-close could dash even the best setup and approach flown by a "high-time" Crusader pilot. Where the Crusader earned accolades, though, was in tactical employment. As the airplane got wider exposure in the fleet, in training and on deployment with the air group, its air combat maneuvering capability began to impress anyone who flew it or opposed it in the air. If any circumstance surrounding Crusader introduction portended a satisfying outcome, beyond the capability of the fighter itself, it was the leadership in the squadrons receiving these new, powerful, yet sometimes temperamental jets. From the earliest days, the Navy regulated a well-honed selection process that moved only the most capable leaders into aviation squadron executive- and commanding-officer billets. When the Crusader arrived, the first squadrons to transition, whether by plan or by happenstance, were led by officers who were a cut above the rest of even that carefully groomed generation of leaders. Crusader transition in those first years of its introduction benefited mightily from this truly exceptional lineup of leaders who modeled the Navy fighter community's best in experience, flying skill, and leadership in the air.

DOGFIGHTING ETHOS

By late 1959, two years into the fleet introduction, those squadrons completing transition on the East Coast (VF-11, VF-32, VF-62, VF-103, and VF-84) and on the West Coast (VF-24, VF-91, VF-142, VF-154, VF-191, and VF-211) were all led by commanding officers who had combat time in World War II in propeller-driven aircraft or Korea in jets, or both: Commanders Prichard, Buhrer, Moorer, South, and Hoppe, then Johnson, in the east and Raehn, Rich, Schindler, Linnekin, Lovegrove in the west. The Marine Corps squadrons transitioning to F8U-1s in those early years (VMF-122 and VMF-312 on the East Coast and VMF-232, VMF-235, and VMF-323 on the West) were commanded by officers of similar experience and character (Lieutenant Colonels Rankin, Gray, Steman, Tooley, and Engel). The Navy F8U squadron executive officers in their eight-to-ten years of flying had logged extensive flight time in earlier jet fighters, and nearly *all* (Lt. Cdrs. Johnson, Stetson, Doolin, Welchel, Stockdale, Snowden, Dankworth, and Hayward) were graduates of the Naval Test Pilot School and had served for at least a while as project test pilots at Pax River, many in the F8U Crusader.

It was this early cohort of leaders in the transition years who—beyond the high performance standards they imposed in air work and squadron tactics; beyond their insistence on superior gunnery; beyond their demonstrated control of the aircraft in high angle-of-attack maneuvering—inculcated in their junior officers as a matter of high priority an indomitable dogfighting ethos. Air superiority was the ultimate objective in every training evolution, in every ready-room chalk-talk, in every meeting of two or more squadron pilots. Any military jet—Marine, Navy, or Air Force—one happened to spot in or near an operating area was fair game to pounce on and "hassle" with to demonstrate one's prowess in the F8U. Transitioning squadron leaders saw it as part of their purpose to train younger pilots solely to maneuver into an enemy's "six o'clock" position, right behind them, within gun range and shoot them down. These engagements with the hypothetical enemy were seen as by nature "complex, three-dimensional affairs that required experience for a pilot to become effective at surviving and killing enemy aircraft . . . [and] in multi-plane engagements at finding aircraft after taking his eyes off of one to evaluate or attack another . . . by participating in hundreds or thousands of practice aerial engagements to become master of the aerial domain. By the nature of their mission and training, F8U pilots were unknowingly preparing for the engagements to come over Vietnam."[14]

The more squadrons that transitioned, the more the dogfighting ethos spread, took hold, and was transmitted to successive generations. It was an identifying characteristic of the Crusader community, from the initial transition to the later years, even as Crusaders were pushed off of flight decks in favor of F-4 Phantoms. That spirit became a badge of merit and an aristocracy of Crusader pilots whenever they encountered Phantom pilots in the Officers Club. Emblematic was the "Mutha" trophy (a name borrowed from a highly restyled passage in the Book of Psalms), awarded annually by the Crusader community to the squadron that most exhibited the most esprit de corps and fighting spirit. Crusader pilots were the rightful inheritors of a gun-shooting legacy that traced directly from the Navy's first ace, Lt. (jg) David Ingalls (who in 1918 sent a Fokker D.VII down in flames with .303-caliber gunfire from his Sopwith) through the Wildcat, Hellcat, and Corsair aces of World War II. Also, it was underwritten to a degree by some clever branding by the Crusader's maker, Chance Vought Aircraft. Advertisements appeared for the "Last Gunfighter," an unmistakable reference to the Crusader's 20-mm cannons and, by implication, the absence of guns on its presumed replacement, the Phantom. Most accounts today point to Paul Thayer, Vought's vice president of sales and a former Navy F4F Wildcat ace, as the originator of that campaign.

That the dogfighting ethos permeated and was kept alive by heirs to the tradition was clearly evident in an account by Bill "Striker" Switzer:

> In my opinion, the F-8 wanted to fly, fight and win every engagement. It was a highly respected,

bad ass machine that wanted to kill the bogey and would if it was flown properly within its performance parameters. The pilot and his Crusader had to think, perform and act as one. The Crusader's gun fighting tactics were definitely unique because it truly was The Last of the Gunfighters with four 20mm cannons for close-in dogfighting. During a Westpac [western Pacific] cruise enroute to Vietnam aboard the USS *Oriskany*, I was part of a section of VF-191 F-8s set to engage Marine F-4's from Kaneohe about 150 miles from Hawaii. As I pre-flighted, I asked our flight deck chief about the somewhat flattened AB [afterburner] tail section. A squadron mate who the night before had a rough high angle-of-attack landing did the damage. The chief said they did engine turns and afterburner checks during the night and couldn't find anything wrong. So, my wingman and I launched for our 2 v 2. Enroute to the engagement, all was good. We picked up the two F-4s and the fight was on. After a few turns we all were in a Lufbery [a circle]. As I tracked the lead F-4 in afterburner I heard on guard [the radio circuit all four aircraft were using], "Navy F-8 behind lead Marine F-4, you are on fire!" I thought this was pretty bold for a Marine to try this trick and I kept the press on. Then he said it again, "No shit, F-8 behind the Marine F-4 you are really on fire." This time I came out of afterburner and looked over the engine instruments for high temps, loss of oil or hydraulic pressure or whatever. Then my wingman said "Striker, you are really on fire." After coming out of afterburner, the fire eventually went out, but was still smoking.

According to NATOPS [see chapter 2], the procedure for a visual [i.e., visible] fire was an ejection. I prepared for an ejection and thought, "I'm getting this baby home." I diverted 150 miles to Hawaii, just waiting for something to happen. Well, this Crusader didn't want to be ditched and I wasn't keen about going for a swim. I made a straight in approach and landed safely with the fire trucks tracking me. The fire actually did go out. Looking at the damage, about eight feet of the lower and mid-section of the afterburner were gone and a few ribs were all that remained. It turned out that due to the hard landing the previous day, one or several of the afterburner's hydraulic nozzle lines had suffered a small leak. When I went into afterburner, the heat ignited the atomized hydraulic fluid and thus, the fire. So, the F-8 was very reliable in this worst-case scenario and designed to stand up, along with the pilot. As said earlier, pilot and his F-8 together, we were always one: confident and damn good.[15]

Lt. (jg) Bill "Striker" Switzer, first-tour aviator and future Blue Angel, stands with a VF-191 Crusader. (Bill Switzer)

GUNS, GUNS, GUNS . . .

In those early years of Crusader transition, the ethos was bolstered by an elite training regimen at El Centro, California, a remote naval auxiliary airfield close to the Chocolate Mountain Gunnery Range. There under the tutelage of the Fleet Air Gunnery Unit (FAGU) top-rated selectees perfected their employment of guns and, for types so armed, missiles. Dan Pedersen, first officer-in-charge of the newly formed Fighter Weapons School, the original "Top Gun," in 1969, recalled, "The F-8 community had learned to dogfight in the FAGU. They were indeed the last of their breed. And boy were they good. The Crusader in the hands of a good pilot, was a world-beater. . The best F-8 guys stayed in the Crusader's envelope [performance boundaries], using their speed and power, where they could dictate the terms of the fight."[16]

For Crusader pilots, the highlight was shooting a towed banner. In three to four weeks of lectures and flying, students learned the latest techniques in air-to-air combat and lessons learned to take back to their own squadron ready rooms. During the Fleet Air Gunnery Meet, an annual competitive event organized in 1956, where squadron commanding officers (COs) brought to their respective squadrons' four top shooters to compete against those of other squadrons. Flight-line signage announced the competition winner as the "Top Gun," a title that foretold the resurrection of the units' mission years later in the exigency of war in Southeast Asia. The irony was that by 1960 FAGU would be disbanded, because it appeared that new missile, radar, and fire-control technologies then coming on line would put an end to the need for close-in aerial combat.

For the Crusader community, that logic did not ring true. Even with the advent of the heat-seeking Sidewinder, Crusader pilots—at least in the early years—viewed gunnery as their forte. Crusader squadrons, in the absence of FAGU, continued regular deployments to gunnery ranges at Marine Corps Air Station Yuma or Naval Auxiliary Air Station Fallon. There F8U pilots routinely flew "high-side," or diving, firing runs at the banner—a 20-by-6-foot nylon mesh sleeve—towed by another aircraft at 20 or 30,000 feet at roughly 200 knots. In the very early years of transition to the Crusader, the reigning West Coast squadron, VF-91, trounced all-comers over multiple trips to the range, scoring altogether hits on the banner numbering iover 100 at 30,000 feet.[17] VF-91 benefited mightily from a gun-oriented leadership team that consisted of a CO who had dispatched three Japanese fighters in air-to-air combat with .50-caliber gunfire, an XO who was a previous individual Battle Efficiency E winner for gunnery on the East Coast as well as gun system evaluator at Armament Test at NATC, and a squadron maintenance officer, Lt. Cdr. Gene West, who focused unrelentingly on keeping gun systems in tip-top shape. VF-91 was redesignated VF-194 in 1963 but sustained its aura with continued high scores through the mid-1960s. By this time, other squadrons were closing in. The "Red Checkertails" of VF-24, under the watchful discipline of the executive officer, Lt. Cdr. Jim Stockdale, shot a section-high, for two-plane banner runs, 177 hits on the banner at Fallon in June 1960.

Gunnery scores, though not the final determinant of the winners of the annual type commanders (here, Commander Naval Air Force Atlantic or Pacific, otherwise AIRLANT and AIRPAC) "Battle Efficiency E" awards, contributed mightily. On the East Coast, that pattern began with VF-84, an early F-8C transition squadron. Winning the day fighter gunnery competition for the Atlantic Fleet in early 1959, the squadron went on to a second-place finish at Yuma that year behind a Marine outfit, VMF-232—also flying the Crusader. VF-84 would take home the AIRLANT "E" for 1960. The next three annual "E" awards went to the marksmen of VF-103 in their F-8Cs.

A VF-91 F-8 departs the waist catapult of the USS *Ranger* (CVA 61). (Lawson Coll., Buehler Naval Aviation Library, NNAM)

VF-91, second West Coast squadron to transition to the Crusader, quickly established a benchmark in aerial gunnery. Commanding officer Mac Snowden (standing, fourth from left) and the previous skipper, Clancy Rich, guided the squadron to the "Battle Efficiency E" two years in a row, thanks in large part to excellence in gunnery. Among the VF-91 sharpshooters, Lt. Dave Morris (kneeling, far left) would command an F-8 squadron, become the second of five aviators to top 3,000 hours in the F-8, and attain flag rank. Lt. Sam Flynn (kneeling, far right), would achieve a MiG-21 kill (flying an F-4J as XO of VF-31) and attain flag rank. Lt. Terry Emery (kneeling, fourth from left), a standout gymnast at the Naval Academy, would perish in an F-8 ramp strike five months after this photo was taken. (Author's collection)

Transitioning to the Crusader a year behind VF-91, VF-24 was laying down its own reputation as one of the premier West Coast squadrons. Here, on its *Midway* deployment in 1959–1960, VF-24 executive officer Jim Stockdale (2nd from left) is flanked by Lt. (jg) Herb Hoffman (far left), Lt. Larry Renner (3rd from left), and Lt. (jg) David Ingalls Jr. (far right), coincidentally the son of the Navy's first gunshooting ace in World War I. (Morrie Lewis)

VF-24 achieved consistently high gunnery scores. Here, shooters on the Fallon deployment of June 1960 kneel in front of their banner, bearing 177 hits. From left, Lt. Bill Lott, Lt. Cdr. Wilbur Sims, VU-7 tow pilot Lt. (jg) Terry Kniffen, Lt. Larry Renner, and Lt. Sam Hubbard. (Morrie Lewis)

Crusader neophytes averaged fewer than ten hits on the banner of total rounds fired in a single run on the banner, each pilot's hits discernible by the color of the smears left by their bullets on the banner. High-timers with years of gunnery experience obtained not many more hits. At least one squadron, VF-191, after the mid-1960s began flying the tow plane down at 5,000 feet, bringing the "high-side" perch down to something less than 10,000 feet. The result was more maneuverability and lower speed, giving more time to hold the gunsight pipper on the banner. Scores shot up. Whereas a typical squadron's total hits on the high-altitude banner would be somewhere in the low one hundreds, VF-191 CO Clyde Tuomela reported squadron scores in the area of two hundred hits.[18] Aside from the early emphasis on banner hits at the range, the gunnery pattern served best to hone mastery of the setup, the "switchology," and familiarity with the sight "picture" and the sound of the guns. What it did not do was replicate the unpredictable twisting and turning at low altitude that was to characterize the MiG encounters to come. High-altitude gunnery "was very reminiscent of a WW2 gun run on a bomber flying straight and level . . . nothing like the real world."[19] Lower-altitude gunnery became more the norm in the late 1960s.

VF-91's gunshooting aura remained in place even after it was redesignated as VF-194. Taking top honors for banner hits in 1964, Lt. Chuck Schroeder and Lt. (jg) M. T. Newell are presented the squadron's symbolic flintlock by the squadron CO, Cdr. Richard Mosley. (Chuck Schroeder)

SHARPENING THE EDGE

Positive reports from early transitioning squadrons, from BuAer field representatives, and from BuAer's own

Pilots of VF-191, "Satan's Kittens," produced a 200-hit aerial gunnery target-practice banner during a deployment to Marine Corps Air Station Yuma, Arizona. More than 30,000 rounds were fired at 27 banners, and nearly 2,000 hits were scored. Top shooters Lt. John Foster and Lt. (jg) Bill Craig are kneeling in front of the banner with the squadron CO, Cdr. Clyde Tuomela. VF-191 was on its way to overtaking VF-194 in gunnery dominance for the year. (Bill Switzer)

functional branches bolstered confidence enough to keep engineering change proposals funded and in train throughout the late 1950s and early 1960s. Word was getting out: naval aviation had a thoroughbred in the Crusader, one that demanded careful grooming with updates. Nose-gear steering, inflight refueling, fitting for Sidewinders, increased wing fatigue-life design, and replacement of the gun-ranging AN/APG-30 radar system with the more capable Magnavox AN/APS-67 for a limited "all-weather" capability were all added to the basic F8U-1 as "in-line block changes to create the F8U-1E.

The APS-67, fitted to some F8U-1Es, provided "continuous scanning of a pie-shaped section ahead of the aircraft up to a range of 16 miles. A cathode ray tube indicator in the cockpit presented detection and range information to the pilot to aid in maneuvering" to a visual acquisition of the enemy aircraft.[20] Externally, the only noticeable change was a new all-plastic radome to accommodate the new radar dish and a small gun-camera window. One hundred thirty F8U-1Es were produced, soon to be passed by the next series upgrade.

When the scope of modifications changed aircraft performance measurably, a new series identifier was warranted. An engine change and ventral fins on the fuselage were sufficient to make the F8U-2, the fourth production F8U-1 serving as the prototype. The -57-P-12 of the F8U-1 and -1E was changed out for the -P-16, adding 500 pounds of additional military thrust that pushed top speed to 960 knots. The additional thrust created more heat in the tail cone. This prompted the addition of cooling intakes at the eleven o'clock and one o'clock positions on the top of the afterburner tail cone section, just aft of four flush-mounted, spring-loaded cooling doors. When airborne, the cooling intakes ingested air naturally "rammed" to high pressure and ducted to lower the afterburner exhaust temperature. When taxiing, the velocity of air into the cooling intakes was not sufficient. Here, negative pressure in the engine bay created by lower power settings forced open the cooling doors to admit outside air to cool the tail cone.

Higher speed exacerbated an already noted tendency to excessive yawing, not just at high altitude but closer to the deck as well. The Crusader had a yaw damper, but as speed increased "oscillations in yaw were amplified at the cockpit location: at maximum speed, the F8U-1 or -1E would 'walk' infinitesimally back and forth under the pilot's butt, giving the impression that airplane was only marginally under control."[21] Without correction, holding a gunnery solution long enough to shoot, particularly at altitude, could be more difficult. An aero-engineering fix came from the flight dynamics engineers, to that bolt two ventral fins onto the lower empennage.

Navy-wide adoption of the Martin-Baker Mark (Mk) 5 ejection seat in 1957 was the occasion for another engineering change to the F8U-2. Originally equipped with a distant cousin of the Douglas Escapac seat, the Mk 5 made zero-altitude (i.e., on the deck or ground) ejection, although the minimum speed for an aircraft in the air at any altitude was 90 knots. The maximum speed in terms of proper seat employment of the seat and pilot survivability was 600-plus knots indicated airspeed.

As for weapons carriage, a new Y-shaped launching rail was developed and incorporated that could mount two Sidewinders on each side of the forward upper fuselage, rather than one Sidewinder per side as in the original configuration. The Y-rack would be routinely integrated on the series that followed the -2, the F8U-2N. VF-84 was the first squadron to receive the new F8U-2 airplane, in April 1959.

THE DEFINITIVE COMBAT MODEL

Even before the F8U-2 made its first flight, with Vought test pilot Konrad at the controls, engineering changes were in flow that coalesced around the -2N series. Avionics technologies were advancing quickly by this time, and expanded mission performance for the Crusader appeared feasible. A radar update, the AN/APQ-83 from Magnavox, with an angle-tracking feature lacking in the APS-67, provided more useful information to the pilot than the APS-67 could for night air-to-air intercepts. To aid the pilot in identifying the target visually once acquired on radar during a night intercept, a Hughes AN/AAS-15 infrared scanner was mounted just forward of the windscreen. The infrared scanner permitted tracking the target on heat alone, without emitting an identifiable radiofrequency (RF) signature.

The rocket pack behind the speed brake was deleted and the newly available space merged into the main fuel cell, extending combat range now out to 394 nautical miles. New avionics demanded more and steady on-demand electrical power, necessitating a new, more powerful generator. A constant-speed drive unit affixed to the engine gearbox drove a new twenty-kilovolt-ampere (kva) generator. Another engine upgrade, from the J57-P-16 to the -P-20, added 1,100 pounds of thrust in afterburner, giving the F8U-2N capability above 70,000 feet. Deliveries began in 1961 to East and West Coast FRSs and to VC-32, VF-111, and VF-154.

At that moment, only one carrier air group, CVG-17, had not yet introduced the Crusader, of any series. CVG-17's fighter squadrons flew McDonnell F3H-2 Demons and Douglas F4D Skyrays. All twelve of the other carrier air groups were deploying with one squadron of Vought F8U-1s, -1Es or -2s to complement their older types (e.g., CVG-10 hosted a Crusader squadron and an F4D Skyray squadron). The contrast between the Demon and Crusader was glaring. The Demon, originally conceived

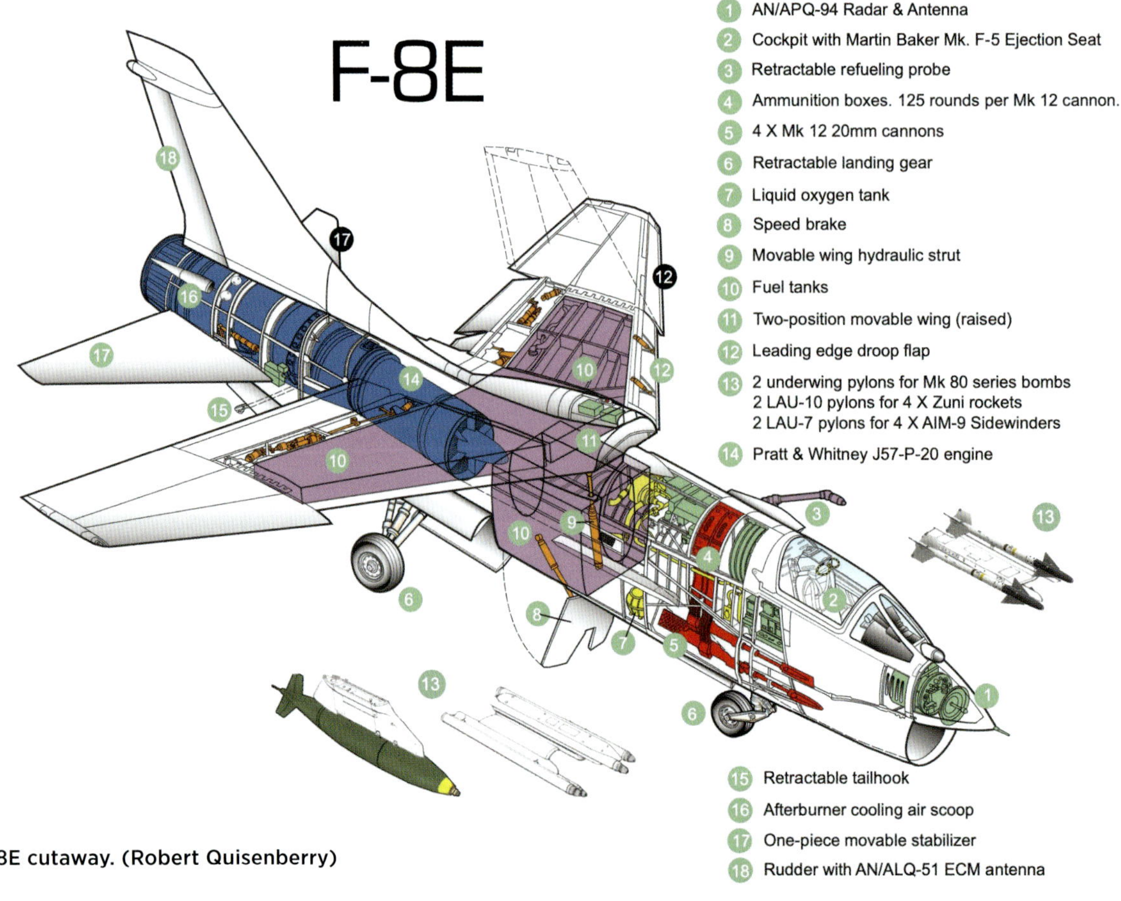

F-8E cutaway. (Robert Quisenberry)

as an interceptor, had been rushed into production a few years before the Crusader as a potential counter to the Soviet MiG-15, then making its appearance in Korea. Even with an engine upgrade to the Allison J71, the Demon had become so overloaded with upgrades that it could barely manage transonic speed. The Demon's days were numbered, whereas the growth capacity of the Crusader begged for another upgrade to round out its mission capability and expand the offensive capacity of the air group.

NATC evaluates weapons-carriage capability of the F-8E during carrier trials. (Buehler Naval Aviation Library, NNAM)

The definitive combat model arrived with the F8U-2NE, which added yet more mission versatility. Another radar upgrade, to the AN/APQ-94, moved detection range out to 30 miles and lock-on at 20. Its larger radar dish meant a slightly modified and larger nose cone. Pylons were added to beefed-up wings to permit carriage of ground-attack weapons that included the two LAU-10 Zuni rocket pods or the Mk 80 series of "iron" (unguided) bombs up to and including the 2,000-pound Mk 84.

Even an AGM-12 Bullpup missile was added to the weapon mix, its guidance avionics housed in a distinctive bump atop the wing center section. Never viewed as operationally practical and ultimately superseded by precision-guided munitions, the Bullpup required the pilot to guide the weapon all the way to the target using a joystick in the cockpit, watching flares on the missile's warhead to line up its flight path with its impact point. For a Crusader pilot trying to maintain speed in a high-threat area and likely "jinking" to avoid ground fire, holding the missile and target in sight all the way to impact was an unnecessary distraction. Early use of the AGM-12 in Southeast Asia was disappointing as well for its inadequate destructiveness against reinforced concrete targets. The missile was never used operationally from the Crusader.[22]

However, the addition of iron bombs on the underwing pylon proved a boon for some missions. VF-191's "Hoss" Pearson recalled, "If we were Flak Suppressors, we carried 2 Mk 84's, one in each wing in addition to the [Side-]Winders. On an Alpha [i.e., large-scale carrier-based attack, so named for the operation plan's 'Appendix A,' in which it was detailed] Strike to Vinh [a coastal city north of the 17th Parallel] as a Flak Suppressor, there was no flak during the bombing runs and as we turned to go feet wet [back out over the sea, to the carrier], a site opened up right below me; I lit the burner and pulled to the vertical, then rolled over and going straight down delivered my two Mk-84's and wiped out the site."[23] The prototype of the new F8U-2NE made its inaugural flight in June 1960, the same month that its forebear, the F8U-2N began deliveries to fleet squadrons.

THE TWO-SEAT TRAINER

The Fleet Introduction Plan was likely the impetus for Vought to take a harder look at a two-seat, lead-in training version of the F8U. If an instructor was in the same airplane as the student, feedback could be more immediate, safety enhanced, and the need for a second chase plane flown by the instructor eliminated. Vought began a conceptual design known internally as the V-408. The overriding design philosophy was to preserve as much commonality with the basic F8U-1 as possible. Inserting a second seat, behind the student, required removal of some equipment forward of the wing leading edge. The second seat had to be raised, to give the instructor pilot a view downward to the student pilot. The top two 20-mm guns on each side were removed, but a single Sidewinder station on each side was retained to give the airplane a representative mission feel. With these changes the takeoff gross weight differed by only an additional 352 pounds, and maximum speed was still close to 1.4 Mach in afterburner.[24] The F8U-1T was briefed to BuAer in the same month that VX-3 was taking the F8U-1 to the *Franklin D. Roosevelt* for its carrier suitability assessment. BuAer moved slowly; naval aviation lacked the resources and funding. That appeared to change three years later, when Vought was encouraged, this time by the Naval Air Training Command, to rework its original plan for a two-seat trainer as an advanced-stage trainer.

Adding a second seat to the Crusader created the F8U-1T. By removing equipment and the top two 20-mm guns on each side, space was made to install the rear seat in an elevated position to provide a view over and down into the forward cockpit. (VFP62.com)

In the interim, Vought's competitors were not idle. Grumman's Cougar was the most prevalent jet fighter on carrier decks in the years immediately after the Korean conflict. The F9F-8 was the most recent version in fleet service but was near the end of its production run when in 1956 the Navy authorized a two-seat prototype. The thinking at the time was that the two-seater could serve as a combat-capable check-out trainer alongside single-seaters in fleet squadrons as well as an advanced trainer in the Naval Air Training Command. The two-seat Cougar never endured in the former role, but the F9F-8T, whose prototype flew in 1956, would go on to serve in the Training Command as the advanced trainer into the early 1970s. In 1958, Grumman's next Navy fighter, the F11F, was deemed less capable than the new F8U-1 and was redirected to the Training Command in 1960 to augment the two-seat Cougars by giving students a "supersonic experience" before their "wings" were pinned on.[25] Most Crusader pilots during the Vietnam War years went through flight training in these two Grumman aircraft.

For Vought, the opportunity to replace both the F9F-8T and F11F with a single supersonic advanced trainer as the primary trainer and primary fleet fighter must have appeared enticing. The original proposal for a two-seat Crusader was reworked and submitted as V-449 in 1961. The Navy authorized funding for one demonstrator, to be built from a modified F8U-1, the 74th off the production line. First flown in early 1962, the F8U-1T was later flown by John Konrad on a tour of Naval Air Training Command bases.

Training Squadron 22 in Kingsville, Texas, was selected to set up a F8U-1T program, starting with a syllabus of four flights for two students with no prior jet time, two students midway through F9F-8T training, and two at the carrier qualification stage. The conclusion was that the F8U-1T, renamed TF-8A (as explained below), was too much airplane for flight students but could be a valuable addition to the RAG syllabus. After a year back at the company, the plane was ferried to Rota, Spain, in March 1963 aboard the USS *Saratoga* and flown to the French base at Istres, where test pilot Bob Rostine made thirty-seven demonstration flights for French Navy officials. After more demonstration flights in England and Italy by test pilot Stuart Madison, the TF-8A was flown to the Paris Air Show, where Konrad, now director of flight operations, wowed the attendees with low-level aerobatic flying.

By October the two-seater was back at Patuxent River to undergo a Navy evaluation that included

The F8U-1T retained two 20-mm guns and two AIM-9 stations for a representative mission "feel." Ultimately, the Navy did not select the two-seat Crusader for series production. (Vought Heritage Foundation)

carrier suitability trials. Meanwhile, production of the Navy's primary attack aircraft, the Douglas A-4 Skyhawk, was nearing its end; there was consternation within Navy leadership about ending the production before the new Vought A-7 Corsair had proved itself. To keep the Douglas line open, a two-seat version, the TA-4, was authorized as the FRS lead-in trainer and as the two-seater for instrument training squadrons on the East and West Coasts. When a decision was finally made regarding a follow-on trainer to replace the F9F-8T, the TA-4 was already in production, had been found less complex to operate and maintain than the F8U-1T, and could be easily converted to a TA-4J.[26]

The 1963 Paris Air Show demonstration drew enthusiasm but no takers. The F8U-1T assumed a new role with the Navy Test Pilot School, then with NASA. Finally, back at Vought, it was used for familiarization training for a foreign Crusader customer, the Philippines. On a training flight from Grand Prairie with a Philippine pilot in the front seat and a Vought test pilot in the rear seat, the engine went through severe compressor stalls and finally quit. Both occupants ejected safely, but the one and only two-seat Crusader was lost in the resulting crash.

Not long before its demise, as mentioned above, the two-seat Crusader was renamed the TF-8A. This was consistent with a new triservice naming convention imposed in 1962. Aircraft designations became standardized among the military services, with the Air Force as executive agent for compliance. Whereas the Navy, from its first acquired airplanes in 1911, had denoted the manufacturer with a letter at the end, the new practice was to hyphenate the type and model and denote by the last letter the series. Henceforth, the *U* denoting Vought manufacture disappeared, and then-existing Crusader type/model/series aircraft were renamed:

F8U-1318	built to	F-8A
F8U-1E130	built to	F-8B
F8U-1P144	built to	RF-8A
F8U-2187	built to	F-8C
F8U-2N152	built to	F-8D
F8U-2NE 286	built to	F-8E

THE FRENCH COME ABOARD

More Crusader series appeared after 1962. One of the few maritime countries other than the United States that in 1962 still operated aircraft carriers was France. The French, when modernizing their force in the early 1960s, naturally gravitated to carrier-capable aircraft for their two carriers, the *Foch* and *Clemenceau*. Both carriers were conventional designs, in that they launched aircraft using catapults and recovered with arresting gear. However, their flight decks were at least twenty feet shorter than those of the smallest U.S. carriers, the *Essex* class.

Updates to the Aquilon, a license-produced version of the British Sea Venom then populating French carrier decks as an interceptor, had taken the late 1940s design as far as it could go. In anticipation of the need, domestic producer Dassault looked at a navalized Mirage, but had not, when the navy concerned itself, engineered approach speeds compatible with the smaller French decks. The French dispatched a study committee to the United States to investigate options. The McDonnell F-4 Phantom was immediately discounted as too large.

F-8E(FN)s of the Aéronautique navale (French naval aviation), here assigned to Flottille 12F, are spotted on the French aircraft carrier *Foch*, next to Dassault Super Étendards, likely belonging to Flotille 14F. (seaforces.org)

A demonstration was conducted with U.S. Navy involvement in March 1962. Two Crusaders from VF-32 embarked on the *Saratoga* made successful landings on and launches from *Clemenceau*. The French needed no more convincing, and an order followed for forty single-seat Crusaders, to be called the F-8E(FN), and six two-seater TF-8E(FN)s. The initial cadre of French pilots was undergoing transition training with the East Coast FRS, VF-174, when the U.S. Navy elected not to produce the F-8 trainer. The French canceled the two-seater buy and added two single-seaters for a total of forty-two aircraft.

NOTES

1. Cdr. William A. Kinsley, "F8U Stars in FIP Program," (Chief of Naval Operations, Washington, DC), *Naval Aviation News* (April 1957), 22–23.

2. Kinsley.

3. Rear Adm. Paul Gillcrist, USN (Ret.), *Crusader! Last of the Gunfighters* (Schiffer Military, 1995), 273.

4. Robert "Crash" Miottel, Interview by Ernest Snowden, 1 April 2024.

5. Mark L. Evans and Roy A. Grossnick, *United States Naval Aviation 1910–2010* (Naval History and Heritage Command, 2016), 302.

6. G. K. Poock, "Trends in Major Aircraft Accident Rates," June 1976, Naval Postgraduate School, Monterey, CA, accessed 19 July 2024 at https://apps.dtic.mil/sti/tr/pdf/ADA027256.pdf..

7. Cdr. Steve "SAM" Marinshaw, USN (Ret.), Interview by Ernest Snowden, 15 July 2024.

8. Capt. Richard Linnekin, USN (Ret.), *Eighty Knots to Mach 2* (Naval Institute Press, 1991), 281–82.

9. Cdr. E. H. Loftin, USN, "Commanding Officer's Endorsement," Memorandum EHL: Ins 5800 Ser: 778, 9 November 1961, National Naval Aviation Museum Archive.

10. Fabio Peña, "USS *Franklin D. Roosevelt* (CVA-42)," *NavSource Online: Aircraft Carrier Photo Archive*, accessed 19 July 2024 at https://www.navsource.org/archives/02/cv-42/42m.htm.

11. Loftin.

12. "Chance Vought F8 Crusader." Flight Safety Foundation, *Flight Safety Network*, accessed 19 July 2024 at https://asn.flightsafety.org/wikibase/type/F8/4.

13. Capt. Robert "Raz" Rasmussen, USN (Ret.), Interview by Ernest Snowden, 7 May 2024.

14. Louis Gundlach, "The Last Gunfighter: F-8 Crusader over North Vietnam," *Hush Kit*, 6. September 2020, accessed May 2024 at https:/hushkit.net/2020/09/06/the-last-gunfighter-analysis-of-f-8-crusader-success-over-north-vietnam.

15. Capt. William "Striker" Switzer, USN (Ret.), Interview by Ernst Snowden, 30 May 2024.

16. Dan Pedersen, *Top Gun: An American Story* (Grand Central, 2020), 47.

17. Al "Lightning" Lansdowne, "Gator Tales," *F-8 Crusader Association*, accessed 19 July 2024 at http://f8crusader.org/gatrtalz.htm.

18. Switzer.

19. Joe Shea, Interview with Ernest Snowden, 18 June 2024.

20. Quoted from Spidle, 130.

21. Linnekin, 265.

22. Spidle, 144.

23. Capt. Larry "Hoss" Pearson, USN (Ret.), Interview by Ernest Snowden, 5 June 2024.

24. Chance Vought Aircraft, "F8U-1T (V-408) Detail Specification," 12 October 1955. NARA, College Park, MD.

25. René Francillon, *Grumman Aircraft* (Naval Institute Press, 1989), 394.

26. Spidle, 120, 124.

F8U-3 with ventral fins extended over the California desert. (NARA)

"THE BEST AIRPLANE WE EVER CANCELLED"?

The F8U was selected by BuAer over McDonnell's competing F3H-G, shown here in mockup in 1954. However, McDonnell was encouraged to refine its design, which evolved into an AH-1 air-to-ground prototype and finally into the F4H prototype, a two-seat missileer, powered by two GE J79 engines, that went on to best the F8U-3 in a fly-off and replace earlier F-8s in the fleet as the Phantom II. (NNAM)

In hindsight, it is plausible to suppose that Vought's F8U-3 derivative was encouraged by BuAer purely as a stalking horse for its preferred supersonic all-weather fighter, McDonnell's F4H-1.

BuAer's practice in the mid-1950s was to bring along a second design in parallel to increase the probability that if one failed for technical reasons, the other could fill the emerging requirement.[1] Vought had reason to play along, as it was also the Navy's practice in this era to field two fighters simultaneously for carrier service with complementary avionics and mission capabilities but with often different powerplants, so as to keep one type flying if engines in the other came down with fleet-wide problems.

MISSILEER TO THE FORE

BuAer's Rear Adm. Robert S. Hatcher, announcing Vought's OS-130 win in May 1953, added, "The competition included at least five designs that could be developed into outstanding service types, although changes to a greater or lesser degree would be required of them all."[2] He had in mind, no doubt, McDonnell's Model 90, a J57-powered concept that came close to Vought's V383 design in some areas of performance. When McDonnell lost to the F8U, the company took stock and did a semiformal survey of views in the Navy top offices—the CNO, the Bureau of Aeronautics, the head of the Fighter Branch, and the Overhaul and Repair depots, really anyone willing to fill out a questionnaire. Once the survey was completed, the company went to work to evolve their Model 90 radically into a supersonic attack aircraft with no less than nine "store stations"—where weapons or sensors could be mounted. The result, the Model 98B, was given a more familiar designation, F3H. McDonnell's unsolicited proposal four months later was assigned the alphanumeric designation, F3H-G, having been submitted as a general-purpose fighter with ground-attack potential to try to move into the design space then occupied by concepts from Grumman and North American. The Navy was impressed with its overall capability and ordered two prototypes, designated AH-1, under a negotiated procurement that permitted McDonnell to circumvent the usual acquisition formalities and avoid the added pressure of industry-wide competition.

In parallel with the OS-130 Supersonic Day Fighter competition and award to Vought, Raytheon had been continuing to refine its Sparrow antiair missile (AAM-N-6), taking it from beam-riding guidance in Sparrow I through active "fire-and forget" radar in Sparrow II (which failed to achieve consistent results) to a semiactive radar-homing seeker in Sparrow III. Raytheon's Sparrow III development was beginning to show favorable results by mid-1955, prompting BuAer to take a second look at its supersonic interceptor for fleet air defense. BuAer's renewed interest in a supersonic all-weather interceptor gained traction now on two promising outcomes: the emerging potential of the Sparrow III and, after fifty hours on a Douglas F4D Skyray test bed, qualification of the General Electric J79 engine in December 1955.

BuAer, assessing the overall capability of the AH-1, encouraged McDonnell to rework it into a supersonic interceptor with hardpoints (attachment points for "stores") and cannons removed. The two prototypes already in preproduction were altered to emphasize the interceptor mission, adding a second seat and Sparrow III–compatible fire control radar. Based on the newly qualified GE J79, the reworked design incorporated dual J79 power plants in lieu of twin J57s. McDonnell's improved Model 98S entered the Navy type/model/series designation system as the F4H-1.

From its plant in Bethpage, New York, Grumman brought forth its G-98 concept, an area-rule, J-65-powered supersonic day fighter design, an earlier attempt to preempt OS-130. Here too, given the comparative maturity of competing designs, BuAer was sufficiently impressed to order three prototypes as F9F-9s, again in a negotiated procurement, in April 1953. Early in preproduction BuAer decided to redesignate these as F11F-1s, and in September 1955 went further and authorized the reengining of two of these with J79 powerplants, those two earning the popular name "Super Tiger." Internally at Grumman, these prototypes were advanced enough to warrant the next series suffix in the line of G-98s, the G-98J. In a short time BuAer began referring to them as F11F-

1Fs. The so-called Super Tiger, briefly known as the F11F-2, appeared to be a capable performer, but the twin-J79-powered F4H-1 outclassed it and was at least a year ahead in maturity. BuAer discussed with Grumman the possibility of a J75-powered version in May 1956, but as measured against the F8U-3 that offered no real gain. BuAer declined to order either F11F variant into production. At that point the F11F-2 reverted to its previous designation, F11F-1F.[3]

Vought's Washington Office staff, in regular dialogue with BuAer and the CNO staff, known as OPNAV, learned enough to alert the company to BuAer's course change for its next procurement to the supersonic all-weather interceptor. Design work had begun in earnest in Grand Prairie by mid-May 1955, just two months after first flight of the XF8U-1. By August 1955 design work had advanced to the point that BuAer formally solicited a bid. In its solicitation to Vought BuAer announced its desire for "the greatest premium on maximum speed over the broadest altitude band, with acceleration and maneuver capability at all altitudes." At a minimum, performance was to include:

- Combat ceiling at least 55,000 feet
- Maximum speed of at least 2.0 Mach
- Combat air patrol endurance of three hours, including combat at 40,000 feet of 15 minutes at military power setting and five minutes in afterburner
- APQ-50 radar with continuous-wave illumination
- Four Sparrow III missiles in submerged (under the aerodynamic outer skin) or semisubmerged carry
- Flexibility for alternative weapons that could include four Sidewinders or four Sparrow Is or Sparrow IIs
- Approach speed of 130 knots
- Spotting of twenty aircraft inside 200 feet of deck

BuAer insisted on operating compatibility with aircraft carrier classes represented by the *Hancock*, *Midway*, and *Forrestal*, using C11–1 catapults and Mk 7 Modification (Mod) 1 arresting gear.[4]

F8U-3 mockup. Note the partially submerged carriage of two Sparrow III missiles, a sharper nose, and very differently shaped intake. (NARA)

VOUGHT'S PROPOSED MODEL V-401

Released internally by Vought engineering on 7 October 1955, then submitted officially five days later with the firm's proposal, Vought's Design Philosophy described concept V-401 as a further development of the F8U family to bring an all-weather complement to the day-night visual-engagement capability of the F8U-1. The V-401 would differ from the F8U-1 only as required for extension of operating boundaries. This meant simply: speed greater than 2.0 Mach and inclusion of the design as new member of a family of aircraft derived from the F8U already in production. That collected all the fighter functions required of carrier-based fighter aircraft. The general layout of the F8U-1 would be retained, with variable-incidence wing and single-piloted cockpit, but repackaged in a noticeably larger airplane to accommodate the J75 engine and weapons. In turn, those mandates meant external changes: large articulating ventral fins for lateral stability at high Mach; a change to the wing planform that moved the outboard section 17.3 inches from centerline for 50 square feet more wing area; a fixed ramp extending from the underside of the inlet for high-pressure ram-air recovery, giving the design a highly raked chin-scoop appearance;

XF8U-3 on flight line. (NARA)

F8U-3 (foreground) and F8U-1 ide by side, showing size difference. (Vought Heritage Foundation)

and a sharper and larger nose radome. The airplane would feature boundary layer control, by which "bleed air" from the engine's compressor was forced over ailerons and inboard flaps to allow slower approach speed, and increased deflection of leading- and trailing-edge flaps. To accommodate the forward embedded Sparrow III station on the lower left of the fuselage, the nose gear was offset slightly to the pilot's right.

In its description of airplane characteristics, Vought presented its V-401 as capable of a combat speed of 2.2 Mach, a combat ceiling of 58,000 feet, and a combat radius of 627 nautical miles. For weapons payload, the F8U-3 would carry three semisubmerged Sparrow III missiles, or alternatively two Sparrow IIIs and two fixed-fin Sidewinders, or potentially four folding-fin Sidewinders internally. The 20-mm guns were deleted from the design.

F8U-3 mockup with extended launchers for Sparrow III missiles. (NARA)

"The most fateful decision made by Vought engineering and concurred in by Vought management in 1955 was that the V-401 would be single place."[5] BuAer asked Vought to include as part of its submission a study of the weight and performance penalties associated with adding a second seat. That study investigated both tandem and side-by-side seating and showed that, holding mission parameters constant, up-and-away performance suffered. Vought insisted that the reduced performance was not offset by a commensurate increase in mission effectiveness. It's fair to surmise that Vought's position on this issue hardened as the design matured past a point where it could be easily changed, without substantial schedule and cost impact. Company leaders may have become less discerning and less inclined to adjust as Navy opinion coalesced in favor of a two-seat design.

In wind tunnel tests, highly adapted models of earlier F8U-family members served as surrogates. A 0.15-to-1 scale F8U-1 model was used in Vought's low-speed tunnel and a 0.02-to-1 XF8U-1 model at MIT's high-speed tunnel. Runs in the high-speed tunnel at 1.99 and 2.5 Mach confirmed that the two-position ventral fins were efficient. Likewise, low-speed runs indicated conclusively that semisubmerged missiles were the most practical.[6]

As had been the practice with earlier XF8U-1 and F8U-1P configurations, V-401 was given the mockup treatment. Mockup construction started in August 1956 in time for an internal Vought review in November and a Mock-Up Board review on 3–5 December. Chaired by Cdr. George Duncan, then head of BuAer's Fighter Design Branch, the Mock-Up Review Board consisted of two other officers from BuAer and three BuAer civilians, among them George Spangenberg, head of the Evaluation Branch. Rounding out Navy participation on the mockup review were Capt. William N. Leonard representing the Deputy CNO for Air and representatives from the Naval Training Device Center and Naval Air Missile Test Center.[7]

BuAer ordered two prototype XF8U-3s BuAer in May 1957 and another sixteen service-test YF8U-3s eight months later. The first XF8U-3 rolled out of the Grand Prairie assembly site in April 1958 and traveled to Edwards AFB in an Air Force C-124 Globemaster. At Edwards, the XF8U-3 went through the same first-flight buildup routine that had been used three years earlier with the XF8U-1. John Konrad, who had become noted for taking the first flight in nearly all of the F8U-series aircraft, was at the controls for the XF8U-3's first flight on 2 June 1958. He took the airplane supersonic on its sixth flight nine days later. Not until mid-August, on the 38th test flight, would Konrad push the airplane past 2.0 Mach. Konrad also flew the second prototype at Edwards, returning to Grand Prairie for the rollout and first flight of the third prototype.

THE FLY-OFF

Physical and performance differences between the F8U-1 and the F8U-3 were significant enough to warrant a full NPE, a Navy Preliminary Evaluation, in the form of a competitive fly-off between the F8U-3 Crusader III (the ultimate in single-engine/single-pilot performance) and the McDonnell F4H-1 Phantom II (a two-engine/two-crewed airplane with near-equal performance). A school of thought and growing body of advocacy for the two-engine and two-crewed interceptor was gaining purchase in OPNAV and in BuAer, mainly due to factors that were coming into clearer focus in the late 1950s: one was that two engines were thought to increase aircraft "get-back" survivability after combat or accident damage, the other that a second operator was needed to hold the semiactive Sparrow III in radar lock all the way to the target, thereby freeing the pilot to handle the aircraft.

Capt. Bob Elder, head of the joint test team for McDonnell's and Vought's entries, climbs out of a Crusader III. (Evergreen Aviation and Space Museum)

At the Naval Air Test Center, teams of test pilots were assigned to one or the other of the two aircraft for the evaluation. All the testers were deeply qualified for the task before them. Lt. Bill Lawrence was the F8U-3 project officer, aided by Bob Ennis from NASA Ames and Lt. Cdr. A. C. O'Neil from the Carrier Suitability Branch. Their counterparts on the F4H-1 were Dick Gordon (future Apollo 12 astronaut) as project officer, Neil Armstrong (future Apollo 11 astronaut) from NASA Dryden, and Lt. Cdr. Bill Nichols from Carrier Suitability. Capt. Bob Elder (awarded the Navy Cross for dive-bombing Japanese carriers at Midway and in 1944 the first naval aviator to fly the early XP-80 jet fighter) assumed the lead for a joint test team aided by Larry Flint (head of Carrier Suitability) and Don Engen (Navy Cross for dive-bombing a Japanese battleship in World War II, a future FAA administrator and director of the National Air and Space Museum), who would take turns flying both airplanes to arrive at a comparative final assessment. Elder, Flint, and Engen all had significant combat flight experience in both World War II and in the Korean War. Now they all prepared to evaluate their respective aircraft on their stand-alone merits and as compared to the other. "This was to be a shoot-out NPE competition, winner take all, and megabucks rode on the outcome."[8]

The test pilot teams left Patuxent River in September 1958 for St. Louis for ground indoctrination in Phantom II systems and performance, followed by two days of similar orientation to the Crusader III in Grand Prairie. By mid-September they were on their way to Los Angeles, from where they would proceed on by car to Edwards for the first phase of NPE flight tests.

Bill Lawrence later remembered that James McDonnell, founder and chief executive of his eponymous company, was very conservative in approach and insisted that when Navy test pilots first flew the Phantom II they not exceed 1.5 Mach. On that first flight Lawrence got airborne in the Crusader III at about the same time that Elder did in the Phantom II. Elder felt constrained to keep his speed below 1.5 Mach; Lawrence ran it out to 2.1 Mach, becoming "the first naval aviator to go twice the speed of sound in a Navy airplane."[9]

In a month of test flying, pilots uniformly commented that the Phantom exhibited unusually high stick forces, particularly in pitch, but that the combined thrust of two J79 powerplants generally overcame any sluggishness. By contrast, the Crusader III was a racehorse, straining at the bit to accelerate beyond 2.0 Mach. Perhaps inevitably, given the design philosophies underlying the two, a consensus was emerging that the Phantom II, with wing-mounted store stations and a second seat for a systems operator, could be best described as a superb multimission missileer, whereas the Crusader III could be best described as a pure high-speed interceptor with excellent handling qualities. In the words of Vought engineering vice president Russ Clark, "The F8U-3 was 5,000 pounds lighter than the F4H-1, used 20 percent

Lt. Bill Lawrence, project officer for the Vought Crusader III. (NHHC)

Bill Lawrence (in pressure suit) surrounded by Cdr. Harry Gibbs, Cdr. Larry Flint, and Vought's Conrad Lau. (NNAM)

less deck stowage space, was 100 knots faster, and had a cockpit set-up into which a new pilot could easily transition from the F8U-2."[10]

The first phase of NPE surfaced pilot gripes that needed to be addressed. For the Phantom II, two problems came to the fore: an engine starter that failed catastrophically on one of Engen's flights, filling the turbine section with debris that could be sucked into the blades; and, second, the high stick forces. The high stick forces were ameliorated early in NPE by adjusting the spring "feel" for the control stick. The starter failure essentially ended the first phase of NPE testing for the Phantom II while a fix to the starter was investigated and the engine was replaced. The starter issue would have to be corrected before the next phase of NPE commenced. As for the Crusader III, the test team rated the prototype as "outstanding" in control response and feel, maximum velocity, rate of climb, and maneuvering at high altitude and high Mach. However, at least one pilot experienced fairly severe engine compressor stalls, the result of the forward-raked intake design failing to regulate properly supersonic air passing the intake lip, exacerbated by a slow-to-respond afterburner nozzle. Pratt & Whitney came up with an automatic bypass control system to balance inlet and exhaust pressure, thereby maintaining a more stable internal pressure condition that mitigated compressor blade stall. For the moment, however, a redesign of the inlet duct engineered by Vought project lead Connie Lau addressed the issue adequately for completion of high-speed tests.[11] In those tests the Crusader III showed itself demonstrably the faster competitor, at 2.2-plus Mach. Yet "many associated with the Vought aircraft were convinced that the Navy had decided on the McDonnell entry before the contest began."[12]

THE DECISION

Captain Elder, with his two project leaders, Dick Gordon and Bill Lawrence, traveled to Washington to brief Vice Adm. Bob Pirie, DCNO (Air), and Vice Adm. Murr Arnold, chief of BuAer, on the results of the initial phase of NPE. The general feeling on the test team was that the Navy would be best served by acquiring both airplanes. The Crusader III was the faster, had easier handling qualities, and was more compliant with the original specification; the Phantom II offered greater growth potential and proved more responsive to the evolved preference for two engines and two crew. Owing largely to pressure from Congress to squeeze savings from fighter procurement, the decision was made to cancel one in favor of the other.

Purely from his BuAer perspective as head of evaluation, George Spangenberg remarked,

> Both airplanes were scheduled for production and were designed with superb programs. Vought did a better job in development than McDonnell, starting a year afterwards with first flight at almost the same time. And Vought did a much better job of fixing things up that showed up in flight test. It was the best flying airplane, best flying fighter at least that the Navy had ever developed according to the Pax [River] reports. Good flight control system. It had better legs. It had higher speed. Climbs were about the same. Ceilings were about the same. You had about a twenty percent cost advantage with the F8U-3. Up to that point in time the Navy had never had less than two fighters in production at the same time. In the normal sense, the F8U-3 won the fly-off. But, in 1957 Congress was screaming . . . and told us to cancel one.[13]

In his first official Evaluation Division assessment, written in February 1958, Spangenberg made these same points, adding, "I am unable to evaluate the relative merits of one versus two engines, or of one versus two seats. Certainly, the F4H is superior in both respects . . . I place a rather low value on both. If a choice must be made, I recommend the F8U-3 for continuance." Nine months later, with results in hand from the second phase of NPE, and with the debate between service advocates of either one or two seats raging more intensely, Spangenberg—in consideration of weapons loadout, flying qualities, maintenance, multimission growth, and operating cost—rated the F8U-3 slightly superior on balance. Then, however, he took on the issue of crew size: "A one-man crew can adequately perform the high-altitude, supersonic intercept mission most of the time with good intercept logic, but the two-man crew can do it better. And, under adverse conditions of high closing speeds, atmospheric conditions or EW [electronic warfare] environments . . . two men are necessary."[14]

On Spangenberg's counsel, the new, incoming BuAer chief, Rear Adm. Robert E. Dixon, recommended to the CNO at the end of November 1958 that the F4H be selected over the F8U-3. The Air Board, a sitting panel of naval aviation flag officers, reviewed the recommendation and advised that the CNO, Adm. Arleigh Burke, accept Dixon's recommendation. Subsequently Burke signed a memo to the Secretary of the Navy informing him of the decision to select the F4H over the F8U-3. In the aftermath, Spangenberg opined, "The day of the single seat fighter is over. Let's not make this mistake again. To develop a whole airplane around that concept, have it turn out to be a better airplane and then not buy it. We shouldn't do that again."[15]

The loss of the F8U-3, announced on 17 December 1958, was a crushing blow to the Chance Vought Company. The setback was amplified by the cancelation of Vought's Regulus II missile program the very next day. Four thousand workers were laid off immediately. Yet, as grim as the news was, the company had a broad enough business base to ensure its viability for the near term. Production was peaking for the F8U-2 and, though not assured in the moment, Crusader production would last at least another five years through a series of modification updates.

CRUSADER III SUNSET

In the wake of F8U-3 cancelation, John Konrad flew in succession the first and second F8U-3s to NASA Langley for sonic boom research, supported by the unfinished fifth production aircraft sent by flatbed truck as a source of spares to keep the first two flying. The third aircraft, flown only nine times in the Navy evaluation, was sent to NASA Ames, with the fourth unfinished

F8U-3 at Wallops Island Flight Test Range for NASA flight tests. (NASA)

aircraft following as its source of spares. The NASA Ames aircraft did not get utilized to any great extent.

At Langley, without the benefit of any procedural publications like NATOPS or flight simulators, Konrad spent two weeks going over his notes to assemble a kind of ground school orientation to familiarize NASA test pilots with normal operating and emergency procedures and unique flying tendencies of the F8U-3. He remained at Langley through two flights each by NASA test pilots Bill Alford and Don Mallick. Konrad monitored their flights by radio to be able to offer recommendations if they encountered any surprises. Flights followed an offshore track that started at Virginia Beach, Virginia, and ended at Chincoteague. Mallick later recalled that on one of those flights he accelerated when abeam of Virginia Beach "and climbed and accelerated to planned altitude and Mach. When stabilized on speed and altitude several minutes prior to passing the sound range—where the sensitive ground microphones measured the pressure wave, or sonic boom . . . on my first flight, the air traffic controller from Norfolk Center asked me, 'NASA, what in the world are you flying?' He was impressed with the aircraft's rapid acceleration and climb—so was I."[16]

Mallick discovered, however, that with so much thrust available, he could not adjust the afterburner; it was either military power "without" or full-on combat power "with." That was a problem for maintaining speed, and he "actually used the speed brake to hold Mach 2.0 for the test point. Otherwise, the airplane would keep accelerating." Both Alford and Mallick observed a five-minute limit at Mach 2.0 to prevent the plexiglas windscreen from softening from heat and possibly blowing in. The ground controller kept a constant watch on the clock to remind the pilots when they were at the five-minute limit and had to slow down.

Compressor stalls that had marred the F8U-3's otherwise impressive Navy evaluation were experienced again by the NASA test pilots, despite the tweaking applied by Connie Lau and his Vought team in NPE. Mallick recalled,

> Both Bill and I experienced stalls and they were startling and dramatic. I can recall one stall I experienced as I accelerated through 1.6 Mach. The engine inlet was located right under the floor of the cockpit, and the stall hit with a loud thump. My feet lifted right off the cockpit floor! This was just the beginning. The inlet started to buzz, shaking and rattling the aircraft as it slowed down. I moved the throttle out of afterburner to the military thrust setting and waited. The F8U-3 had to slow to 0.9 Mach before the engine stall cleared. Fortunately, engine temperature did not seem to be a problem and I did not have to shut the engine down.[17]

The NASA sonic boom investigation wrapped up in October 1958. The airplanes were stored and eventually broken up.

NOTES

1. The chapter title is from Spangenberg, Interview by Rausa.

2. Butler, 182.

3. Francillon, 378–81.

4. Chance Vought Aircraft, "F8U-3 (V-401) Design Philosophy: Engineering Report 9874," 7 October 1955, NARA, College Park, MD, 6.

5. Tommy Thomason, *Vought F8U-3 Crusader III: Super Crusader* (Steve Ginter, 2010), 13.

6. "F8U-3 (V-401) Design Philosophy," 6.

7. Chance Vought Aircraft, "Guide to F8U-3 Mock-Up," 12 October 1955, NARA, College Park, MD.

8. Vice Adm. Donald D. Engen, USN (Ret.), *Wings and Warriors: My Life as a Naval Aviator* (Smithsonian Institution Press, 1997), 211.

9. Vice Adm. William P, Lawrence, USN (Ret.), Interview by Paul Stillwell, 24 September 1990, Oral History Program, U.S. Naval Institute photo archive.

10. Robert F. Dorr, "F8U-3 Crusader Was Really Hot Might Have Been," *Defense Media Network*, 17 November 2012, accessed 19 July 2024, https://www.defensemedianework.com/stories/f8u-3-crusader-was-really-hot-might-have-been/.

11. Thomason, 72–73.

12. Dorr.

13. Spangenberg, 131–33.

14. Thomason, 77–79.

15. Spangenberg, 133.

16. Don Mallick, *The Smell of Kerosene: A Test Pilot's Odyssey* (National Aeronautics and Space Administration, 2003), 85.

17. Mallick.

CRUSADERS IN EARLY FLEET ACTION

The Cuban Missile Crisis is today regarded as a defining moment in the presidency of John F. Kennedy. When the Soviets began uncrating nuclear missiles and nuclear-capable bombers on the island of Cuba in the summer of 1962, Kennedy pushed back and exposed the Soviet's provocation, ultimately calling their bluff.

Flight-deck personnel attach the catapult launching bridle on an F-8E from VF-51, commanded by Cdr. James Stockdale. The photo was taken just weeks before VF-51 and Air Wing 5 were assigned to Operation Pierce Arrow in early August 1964. (Lawson Coll., Buehler Naval Aviation Library, NNAM)

Less well remembered is the large-scale redeployment of U.S. naval forces that backed the president's play. The U.S. Second Fleet delivered the leverage needed for interdiction and also gave the president a means for obtaining accurate, low-level, near-real-time intelligence. That asset was RF-8As (formerly F8U-1Ps, renamed in July 1962 under the joint redesignation system) from NAS Cecil Field, backed up by photo Crusader detachments on the *Enterprise* and *Independence*, steaming offshore. The photo intelligence capability of the RF-8As was augmented by six gun-fighter F-8Ds (formerly F8U-2Ns) at Key West when on 28 September they were "chopped" (change of operational commander) to the Air Force under the North American Air Defense Command. Navy gunfighter F-8s were supplemented by Marine F-8s when VMF-122 arrived in NAS Key West.

Lt. (jg) Bruce Wilhelmy confers from the cockpit with Chief Photographer's Mate M. D. Marbut. Wilhelmy flew on VFP-62 commanding officer Cdr. Bill Ecker's wing in the first RF-8 mission over Cuba. (VFP62.com)

OPERATION BLUE MOON

Tensions escalated quickly on the evening of 14 October, when high-altitude imagery from a U.S. U-2 confirmed the presence of SS-4 medium-range and SS-5 intermediate-range ballistic nuclear missile sites under construction. Kennedy demanded their withdrawal. On 22 October he ordered a naval blockade of Cuba by the Second Fleet. To make the strongest public case for the blockade in the face of Soviet denials, sharper photographic evidence was needed. While U-2 imagery showed indications of Soviet activity, the grainy high-altitude scenes were indecipherable to all but a small cadre of photo interpreters. Greater detail and resolution were vital if the United States was to make a convincing case in an international forum. Only Navy and Marine RF-8As could deliver the fidelity the situation demanded.

The Navy's VFP-62, augmented with four pilots from Marine squadron VMCJ-2, was tasked with overflying a hostile Cuba to bring back the evidence, under the codename Blue Moon. Ten jets were allocated to the mission, four of those on four-hour alert at Key West. RF-8As made at least two flights daily, in pairs, from NAS Key West, beginning 23 October.[1] The first section of two airplanes was led by squadron CO Cdr. William Ecker, with Lt. Bruce Wilhelmy on his wing. Ecker and Wilhelmy crossed the Florida Strait in just fourteen minutes at a 400-knot clip. Skirting the Havana skyline, they banked west and headed for the suspected missile assembly and storage at San Cristobal, Cuba, which

Lt. Gerry Coffee (left) and Lt. Arthur Day confer with Rear Adm. Joseph Carson, commander of Fleet Air Jacksonville, about their first Blue Moon mission. Coffee would later be shot down over North Vietnam piloting an RA-5 and be held prisoner for seven years. (VFP62.com)

they planned to overfly. Over San Cristobal, as the cameras rolled, they saw antiaircraft gunners running to their gun emplacements. Ecker remembered, "You could see the popcorn in your mirrors," referring to puffs of flak, "but, we never got hit."[2]

This flight and subsequent missions returned by way of NAS Jacksonville, where the film canisters were downloaded and taken into VFP-62's Fleet Air Photo Lab for processing and analysis. The photo Crusaders then returned to Key West for their next overflight missions by way of Cecil Field if the airplanes required a squadron-level fix. Pilots were under strict orders that, if their aircraft were fired on and resulting damage forced an emergency landing, they were to contact Guantanamo Naval Base by prearranged signal for fighter escort and then land at Guantanamo. If damage was such that landing at Guantanamo was not possible, the pilot was to eject over the sea so that the airplane could not be recovered by Cuban or Soviet forces.[3]

Aviation Boatswain's Mate Third Class Lee Perrin (*left*) and Avionics Technician Third Class Eric Nelson, both with VFP-62, button up panels covering an RF-8A's camera bays for the next mission. (VFP62.com)

F8U-1P takeoff. (NARA)

Following Ecker's first flight, the developed film was rushed to the National Photographic Interpretation Center, which was

> a secret facility occupying an upper floor of a Ford dealership in a derelict block at Fifth and K streets in Northwest Washington. Half a dozen analysts pored over some 3,000 feet of imagery to confirm the disposition of nuclear weapons loaders, launchers and the missiles themselves. Ecker was called to Washington to personally brief the Joint Chiefs. At ten o'clock the following morning, CIA analysts showed President Kennedy stunningly detailed photographs that would make it crystal clear that Soviet leader Nikita Khrushchev had broken his promise not to deploy offensive weapons in Cuba.[4]

The next day, the same photographs were in New York, where on 25 October the American ambassador to the United Nations, Adlai Stevenson, presented them as undeniable proof of Soviet malfeasance and deception. The confrontation between superpowers grew especially tense in the ensuing days; VFP-62 flew its greatest number of sorties—fourteen—on 27 October. That day, an Air Force U-2 was shot down by the Cuban military. An intense effort was mounted to pinpoint the source of the surface-to-air missile launch for possible strikes. Reprisals were called off when, on 28 October, the Kremlin, bowing to inevitably narrowing op-

Low-level photo of San Cristobal medium range ballistic missile site No. 1, showing missile shelters, fuel tank trailers in lower left, and mobile oxidizer tanks in lower left, with missile erector under a tent in upper middle of the photo, and missile erector, taken on 23 October 1962 by Commander Ecker. (VFP62.com)

Low-level photo taken on 23 October by Commander Ecker of San Cristobal site showing five missiles under covers. Foreground is a missile preparation tent. (VFP62.com)

Navy Unit Commendation presented by President John F. Kennedy to VFP-62 on 26 November 1962, accepted by VFP-62's commanding officer, Cdr. William Ecker. (VFP62.com)

VMCJ-2 RF-8A over Cuba on the first day the Marines flew wing on VFP-62. Photo was taken on October 25 from a VFP-62 RF-8A. Blue Moon missions were normally flown in pairs. (VFP62.com)

tions, agreed to remove its missiles. VFP-62's overflights continued until 15 November to confirm that missiles and bombers were being crated for removal.

One such overflight was assigned to Lt. Cdr. Tad Riley. Riley and his wingman, Capt. Fred Carolan from VMCJ-2, observing radio silence, penetrated Cuban airspace on 5 November to document the travel of a disarmed missile. The missile was making slow progress by truck over back roads from the missile site at Sagua La Grande to the south coast port of Cienfuegos for removal from Cuba. At one point, descending to 50 feet at 600 knots, Riley quickly found himself passing over a surface-to-air missile site and was relieved by the absence of any radar tracking indication. Turning southwest toward the last reported position of the heavily laden truck, Riley was startled by a radio transmission that warned, "MiGs at nine o'clock."

He scanned left and was unpleasantly surprised to see a MiG-21 angling toward him. There had been no mention of the presence of MiG-21s in his preflight brief, and he felt more than little consternation as hewent to military power, put in left rudder, and pulled hard on the stick. Holding 6 ½ g's in his turn, he craned his head around enough to see the MiG "pulling lead" (turning faster and pulling even) and closing on him. He heard himself mutter, "This guy is really good."[5]

He moved his throttle past the detent to engage afterburner and tightened his turn to 8 g's. The MiG started to overshoot. In the next few split seconds, Riley knew his RF-8 had given him a small margin to try another move. He quickly reversed his turn and unloaded (relaxing the back-pressure he was holding on to the control stick, trading lift for speed), heading for the cover of high grass and low trees below. Soon he was streaking along just a few feet above the lowest treetops at 1.1 Mach. The MiG was falling farther behind, but his Crusader, at high speed over unevenly heated ground, was exhibiting its characteristic tendency for yawing in irregular and uncomfortable sideslips. One more ridgeline remained before his Crusader would go "feet wet" over the deep blue of the Florida Straits. Along the ridgeline he spotted a break in the tree line on the crest and made for it. Approaching at no more than ten feet and still clocking over 1.0 Mach, he spotted a local campesino leading his burro over the crest. The Crusader, passed over the man before its sound arrived, but no doubt the following shock wave knocked the unsuspecting farmer senseless. As Riley went feet wet, he caught sight of his wingman and the two proceeded north at wavetop height until the MiG broke off.

So crucial to the U.S. position on the world stage throughout crisis was the intelligence provided by the RF-8As, that after the crisis subsided the president made a point of recognizing their contribution personally. With the squadron formed up in front of their aircraft, the president presented VFP-62 the Navy Unit Commendation. Twelve Navy pilots and four Marine pilots received the Distinguished Flying Cross. The RF-8A would be called on again in less than two years, and halfway around the globe, to deliver the high-fidelity photographic imagery so prized by the national command authorities—this time in Southeast Asia.

OPERATION YANKEE TEAM

The nations of Southeast Asia were in 1964 an increasingly unstable collection of monarchies, parliamentary coalitions, and dictatorships beset by national-front movements aiming to depose the old regimes. Communist-allied insurgencies agitated for wars of national liberation with increasing violence, abetted from outside the region by avowed Marxist governments. In South Vietnam American advisors, who had been on the ground for almost a decade and now numbered 16,000, were aiding the South's resistance to North Vietnamese incursion and to the Viet Cong insurgency.

Laos, in the heart of the region, was nominally governed by a coalition of parties that was undone on 17 May 1964 when communist Pathet Lao forces escalated their attacks on the government. The situation was critical by the end of the day: the Pathet Lao was overrunning an area in eastern Laos that would encompass what would later be known as the Ho Chi Minh Trail. This was viewed as a dangerous escalation that risked outflanking U.S. interests in South Vietnam. Twenty-four hours later, Carrier Task Group 77.4 was alerted to prepare for reconnaissance flights over Laos and directed to move to the entrance of the Gulf of Tonkin. The JCS authorized the first reconnaissance flights to be flown over the Plain of Jars in Laos, in Operation Yankee Team. A continuous, daily program of reconnaissance flights was implemented, with CTG 77.4 carriers rotating through Point Yankee—16 degrees north and 110 degrees east. First on the scene

RF-8A over North Vietnamese terrain similar to what Lt. Charles Klusmann passed over on his last mission to Laos. (NARA)

was the USS *Kitty Hawk*, launching her first photo reconnaissance flight on 18 May.[6]

Three days later, Lt. Cdr. Ben Cloud and wingman Lt. Charles Klusmann both from VFP-63 Det C, launched in their RF-8A photo Crusaders, flying west-northwest 500 miles over northern South Vietnam and penetrating Laotian airspace. Both pilots "noticed white puffs blooming around their planes and red streaks rising from the ground."[7] Klusmann's RF-8A was hit, and his left wing began to burn. Both climbed to altitude and headed to sea. The flames subsided but Klusmann lost pieces of the wing all the way down to the *Kitty Hawk*'s recovery pattern. Klusmann landed aboard the *Kitty Hawk* with only 600 pounds of fuel remaining but unharmed.

Two weeks later, Klusmann was scheduled to make a run along Route 7 between Khang Khay and Ban Ban in central Laos. His wingman on this mission was Lt. Jerry Kuechmann. From 1,500 feet at 550 knots, the landscape below seemed a blurred, unremarkable pattern of irregular green paddies. Though Klusmann saw no tracers or flak bursts, he soon felt several distinct thumps—37-mm ground fire hitting the wing and fuselage. The hits took out PC-1 and PC-2 hydraulic systems, powering flight control surfaces on both sides. In less than two minutes Klusmann's plane was not responding to control stick inputs, and it was time to leave the airplane. The Martin Baker seat worked as advertised. Pulling the face curtain down over his mask initiated a series of steps that unfolded in a split-second sequence: shoulder restraints jerked him back into the seat, leg restraints pulled his calves into the front of the seat to prevent flailing, and the canopy left the airplane. A controlled explosive charge under the seat then propelled seat and pilot upward on twin steel rails that guided the seat's exit from the cockpit. The seat had traveled six feet up those rear rails when a lanyard triggered a rocket motor that blasted Klusmann, still in his seat, away from the airplane. In just over two seconds, drogue parachutes stabilized his seat and extracted the main chute. In the few minutes of his descent under the parachute canopy, Klusmann glimpsed his RF-8A impact the ground and explode. The scene was surreal.

He was snapped out of his reverie by the sound of bullets whizzing past his head. The chute drifted into a tree. The impact badly strained a hip and sprained a knee and ankle, causing Klusmann when he was free of the seat to alternately limp and crawl toward the nearest cover. His wingman orbited overhead until he was down to "bingo fuel," just enough to get to the *Kitty Hawk*, and had to make for the ship. An hour later an H-34 helicopter flown by Air America, a Central Intelligence Agency operation, arrived and immediately drew ground fire. that seriously wounded the copilot. The helo was punctured by at least 80 hits but returned vigorous fire. Klusmann realized that the Pathet Lao could well bring down the helo if it hovered any longer and waved them off. Klusmann was then overwhelmed by Pathet Lao insurgents and became a prisoner. After enduring eighty-six harsh days in captivity, he managed to escape and make his way to a remote Air America base.

He took back with him accounts of his treatment at the hands of the enemy that influenced evasion and escape training for the intensifying conflict.[8] Klusmann was the first naval aviator to be captured by the enemy in Southeast Asia. The day after his shootdown armed escorts became the rule, but the following day an F-8D escorting a RF-8 over Laos was taken down by ground fire. The pilot was rescued. Klusmann would not for long be the lone naval aviator captured by communist forces. Two months later another one, Everett Alvarez would be taken prisoner, this time in Vietnam during Operation Pierce Arrow.

Lieutenant Klusmann is welcomed after his escape and return from captivity by Adm. Ulysses S. Grant Sharp, Commander-in-Chief Pacific, and Vice Adm. Roy L. Johnson, Commander Seventh Fleet. (NHHC)

OPERATION PIERCE ARROW

After a high subsonic crossing of 300 miles of open ocean, four F-8Es arrived over the embattled destroyer USS *Maddox* (DD 731) in the late afternoon of 2 August 1964. The *Maddox* had taken three North Vietnamese P-4 motor torpedo boats under fire minutes before the F-8s arrived, and now, with orders to attack and destroy the threatening P-4s, the Crusaders opened fire on the retiring boats with Zuni rockets and a 20-mm cannon.

Crusaders of Air Wing 5 had been exercising over the USS *Ticonderoga* (CVA 14) when the urgent call for backup came in. The first two-plane section of Crusaders, led by VF-51 squadron commander Cdr. James Stockdale, was joined by a second two-plane section led by VF-53's XO, Cdr. Robair Mohrhardt. In their first and only firing pass, Stockdale's wingman reported damage from a presumed hit by small-arms fire. (The wingman diverted to Da Nang, where it was determined that the aircraft had not been hit as thought; the pilot had failed to retract the F-8's wing droop prior to the high-speed transit, resulting in a rather severe jolt.) Meanwhile, Cdr. Mohrhardt and his wingman sank one boat with 20-mm gunfire and damaged the other two before the Crusaders returned to the *Ticonderoga*.

Three days later, President Lyndon B. Johnson ordered retaliatory strikes on North Vietnamese torpedo boat bases and oil storage facilities. Stockdale led four VF-51 F-8Es from the *Ticonderoga* as strike escort and flak suppression for the air wing's A-4 bombers, which hit an oil storage tank at Vinh. Mohrhardt led seven VF-53 F-8Es escorting a strike group attacking P-4 bases at Quang Khe and Ben Thuy.

This was only a foretaste of the intense aerial contest that would play out over Vietnam for the next decade. Early in those ten years the F-8 Crusader would seal its reputation as the preeminent dogfighter, only to have its service abbreviated as the F-4 Phantom was introduced in greater numbers. Indeed, by the start of

In the days immediately following Operation Pierce Arrow, a Pacific Fleet photographic unit was assigned to obtain reenacted documentary coverage of the units involved. Here aviation ordnancemen arm a VF-53 F-8E with Zuni rockets aboard the USS *Ticonderoga*. (NHHC)

Operation Rolling Thunder in March 1965, 60 percent of fleet fighter squadrons on the East and West Coasts had already transitioned to the Phantom. As for the two section leaders in Operation Pierce Arrow, both came to their roles that day with significant Crusader experience: after teaching at the test pilot school, Stockdale had progressed through duty as maintenance and operations officer of an early F8U squadron, VF-211; as executive officer of VF-24; and finally to command of VF-51, becoming the first F-8 pilot to accumulate more than 1,000 hours in the airplane. Mohrhardt had ninety-five combat missions flying Grumman Panthers in Korea, and by the end of the decade was officer-in-charge of a carrier-borne detachment of RF-8A photo reconnaissance Crusaders. By 1964 Mohrhardt was executive officer of F-8E squadron VF-53, "fleeting up" as commanding officer the next year. Mohrhardt's VF-53 would become the first F-8E squadron to fly more than 1,000 combat hours in a month, March 1966.

NOTES

1. Cdr. Peter B. Mersky, USN (Ret.), *RF-8 Crusaders over Cuba and Vietnam* (Osprey/Del Prado, 2001), 9.

2. Capt. William B. Ecker, USN (Ret.) and Kenneth V. Jack, *Blue Moon over Cuba: Aerial Reconnaissance during the Cuban Missile Crisis* (Osprey, 2013, Kindle).

3. Joseph V. Charyk, Director NRO, "Interdepartmental Cover Support to Operation Blue Moon," National Reconnaissance Office, accessed 15 June 2024, http://www.cia.gov/readingroom/docs/.

4. Michael Dobbs, "The Photographs That Prevented World War III," *Smithsonian Magazine* (October 2012), accessed 15 June 2024 at https://www.smithsonianmag.com/history/the-photographs-that-prevetned-world-war-iii-36910430/.

5. Lt. Cdr. Tad Riley, USN, Interview by Paul Gillcrist, 1995, 78–81.

6. Col. Edward Burtenshaw, USAF, "Project Current Historical Evaluation of Counterinsurgency Operations (CHECO)," Hickam AFB, HI: PACAF, 8 March 1966, accessed 10 June 2024, https://apps.dtic.mil/sti/pdfs/ADA486857.pdf.

7. Edward J. Marolda, "Survival, Evasion, Resistance & Escape," *Naval History* Magazine (April 2024), accessed June 2024 at https://www.usni.org/magazines/naval-history-magazine/2024/april/survival-evasion-resistance-escape..

8. Capt. Charles F. Klusmann, USN (Ret.), Interview by Ernest Snowden, 30 April 2024.

THE VIETNAM AIR WAR

VMF(AW)-212 F-8E from the *Oriskany* pulls up past a Viet Cong position ten miles southwest of Hué smoking from hits by 2.75-inch rockets, 12 November 1965. (NHHC)

Operation Pierce Arrow came to represent only a first application of naval airpower in an ever-deepening involvement by Pacific Fleet carrier air wings in Vietnam. Attacks by communist insurgents in South Vietnam intensified in the months that followed, fueled by a flow of men and materiel across the 17th Parallel from North Vietnam. Operation Flaming Dart I, an alpha strike against North Vietnamese army barracks on 7 February 1965, was put into motion after a mortar attack that killed eight Americans. A second Flaming Dart strike, ordered four days later, hit another troop barracks after another mortar attack killed twenty-three Americans. F-8Es and F-8Cs of *Hancock* squadrons VF-211 and VF-24, respectively led off with flak suppression. *Coral Sea* squadron VF-154 flew escort, losing an F-8D flown by Lt. Cdr. Robert Shumaker to 37-mm antiaircraft. Shumaker became the second naval aviator captured in Vietnam, and second-longest-held prisoner in the North.

OPERATION ROLLING THUNDER

In Washington, D.C., a conceptual strategic "firewall" related to holding the communist advance in check was at risk of collapse. President Johnson had already issued National Security Action Memorandum (NSAM) 273, a statement of elevated concern and focus by his administration on the festering problem of Vietnam. NSAM 288 followed on 17 March 1964, codifying a stepped-up role for the United States in protecting the Saigon government. To undergird NSAM 288 with force, the Joint Chiefs of Staff tasked Commander-in-Chief Pacific (CINCPAC) to prepare an action plan for graduated military pressure designed to interdict the flow of materiel to communist forces in South Vietnam. CINCPAC Operation Plan (OPLAN) 37-64 outlined a campaign for reducing key communist war-making infrastructure already established in parts of the South and the panhandle of southern North Vietnam. To the plan was appended a target list of ninety-four railyards, bridges, and oil storage installations to be allocated for attack to U.S. Air Force and U.S. Navy aviation commands under Operation Rolling Thunder, which would begin on 2 March 1965. The target list became the organizing construct for alpha strikes (chapter 4). Navy and Marine F-8 Crusaders were drawn into the campaign from ships at sea and bases ashore at Da Nang for strike escort, flak suppression, close air support, and combat air patrol.

Prosecution of the air war in South Vietnam was largely the province of Marine Corp aviation, in support of Marines on the ground in direct contact with Viet Cong (VC) insurgents. Marine F-8Es arrived during 1965 as the fighter complement of Marine Air Group 11, flown by the VMF(AW)-312 "Checkerboards." The Checkerboards managed 718 combat missions in the South, mostly in direct support, until deactivated two months later. The "Death Angels" of VMF(AW)-235 arrived at Da Nang that month with F-8Es to relieve them. The F-8E, with underwing pylons, was used extensively with Mk 80–series bombs in the South and occasionally on targets north of the 17th Parallel. It was on one of the latter excursions, on 11 November 1966, that Capt. Orson Swindle was shot down in his F-8E to become another of the longest-held prisoners in North Vietnam.

The Death Angels were relieved as MAG-11's F-8E squadron by the VMF(AW)-232 "Red Devils" in November 1966, who arrived in increments at Da Nang over a three-month period. By the end of December 1966, VMF(AW)-232 had flown 571 sorties and dropped 418 tons of ordnance on VC targets. Four of their aircraft had been hit by small-arms fire but made it back to Da Nang safely. Maj. Ed Townley became the first Red Devil to be shot down by ground fire on 4 May 1967, as he circled a suspected enemy position. He pointed the Crusader out to sea and ejected, to be picked up and returned to Da Nang. By the end of June two more Crusaders and their pilots had been lost, one to enemy fire and one to mechanical failure. Then, on 15 July, two more airplanes were destroyed in their revetments by Viet Cong rocket fire.

The Red Devils were relieved by the VMF(AW)-235 Death Angels, who returned with their F-8Es in February 1967. In February 1968, the Death Angels saw intensive action in direct support of Marines besieged at Khe Sanh. For three weeks, the squadron dropped napalm and strafed VC positions with 20-mm gunfire. They dropped 2,000-pound Mk 84 bombs from underwing pylons as close as 300 yards to friendly lines so as to collapse tunnels the VC were digging to approach the outer barbed-wire defensive perimeter, to seal off the Marines' front line behind a protective barrier against tunneling sappers. By May the squadron was retired to the Marine Corps Air Station in Iwakuni, Japan, for reconstitution as an F-4J squadron.

A fourth Marine Crusader squadron to serve in Viet-

Marine F-8E of VMF-235 prepared for a close-air-support mission, armed with Zuni rockets and Mk 82 general-purpose bombs mounted on a multiple ejector rack carried on the inner wing pylon, at Da Nang in April 1967. (ALAMY)

Marine F-8E of VMF(AW)-212 positioned on the USS *Oriskany's* catapult No. 1. (NARA)

nam was actually deployed with the Navy's Air Wing 16 in the *Oriskany* (CVA 34), substituting for a Navy fighter squadron that was transitioning to F-4Bs. After workups with the air wing, the *Oriskany*, with the VMF(AW)-212 "Lancers" aboard arrived at "Dixie Station" off South Vietnam in May 1965 and attacked targets of opportunity for two weeks to acclimate to combat operations before moving north to "Yankee Station." By midsummer, the Lancers' F-8Es had been modified to carry all Mk 80–series bombs on their underwing pylons, which opened up greater means for taking down reinforced structures. On 17 October, the Lancers dropped the Vu Chua railroad bridge using 2,000-pound Mk 84s. Three weeks later, the Lancers were using the same ordnance against the Hai Duong bridge when Capt. Harlan Chapman's F-8E, last off the target, was shot down; he became a prisoner of the North Vietnamese. Another F-8E, flown by Capt. Ross Chaimson in attacks on the same bridge two weeks later, was damaged by ground fire, forcing Chaimson to eject; he was rescued at sea. On 9 September, their CAG (air wing commander, the abbreviation retained after air groups became air wings in 1963), Commander Stockdale, was shot down and became a prisoner of the North Vietnamese. On that mission Lt. Col. Charles Ludden, USMC, CO of the Lancers, was severely wounded and his Crusader badly damaged, but he brought his F-8E back to the ship to receive later his third Distinguished Flying Cross and Purple Heart. As senior squadron commander in CVW-16 in the absence of Stockdale, Ludden assumed temporary command, in one of the rare instances where a Marine commanded a Navy air wing—let alone one consisting of four Navy squadrons. In November, the *Oriskany* was taken off the line, and Lieutenant Colonel Ludden took his squadron back to Marine Corps Air Station Kaneohe, Hawaii. For his outstanding performance in command of the Lancers and temporarily of CVW-16, Ludden was presented the Alfred Cunningham Award as Marine

VF-111 traded its F-8Ds for F-8Es for its third combat cruise, this time aboard the *Oriskany* in 1966. Of note, on this cruise Dick Schaffert (standing, second from left) battled four MiG-17s, joined by two more MiG-21s, in a single ten-minute engagement that is still studied today as a prime example of the F-8 flown to its full combat potential. Foster "Tooter" Teague (standing, third from right) in his next assignment would get an opportunity to evaluate the MiG-21's performance in a secret project known as Have Doughnut, then back in Southeast Asia score his own MiG-17 kill flying the F-4J. U.S. Air Force exchange pilot Capt. Wilfred Abbott (standing, sixth from right) would unfortunately be downed by MiG-17 cannon fire on this cruise and remain in captivity in Hanoi until 1973. (NNAM)

An F-8D of VF-111 from the USS *Midway* presses a run on a target in South Vietnam on 3 October 1965. (NNAM)

Aviator of the Year.

For Navy Crusaders, Rolling Thunder meant conventional escort, flak suppression, and combat air patrol integral to alpha strikes into North Vietnam and for fleet defense offshore. In shorter, unscripted missions and "cyclic" (continuous and regular) operations were the rule. In cyclic ops, in comparison to planned alpha strikes by all or most airwing assets available on particular targets, generally fewer aircraft were involved and targets—chosen, essentially, from whatever was in reach at the time—were more random in nature and often fleeting in duration. In modernized *Essex*- and *Midway*-class carriers, the air-wing fighter component of most alpha strikes into North Vietnam comprised two F-8E or F-8C squadrons (the *Midway* and *Coral Sea* (CVA 43) each had one F-8D squadron early in the campaign), as well as detachments that included RF-8s for pre- and poststrike reconnaissance.

Initially, ground fire, in every caliber from 23-, 37-, 57-, and 85- to 100-mm, presented the most pernicious threat faced by Crusaders and their charges, the A-4 Skyhawks. When strike airplanes made their low-altitude pullouts, they were exposed not just to larger calibers but small-arms barrages as well. By early 1965 the North Vietnamese may have had around a thousand heavy-caliber guns throughout the country. By the end of the year, the number quadrupled. In the early years of Rolling Thunder F-8s often flew a particular profile to suppress flak: a 45-degree roll-in from 8,000 to 10,000 feet to salvo (fire all of) a Zuni rocket payload at 4,500 feet, pulling the nose up about five mils on the gunsight to squeeze off 20-mm gunfire, saturating the area around the Zuni impact points. When the descent reached 3,000 feet the pilot initiated a pullout, but the Crusader might not actually begin to climb before it was down another 1,000 feet, into small-arms range then passing upward through the ranges of heavier-caliber guns. In the first ten months of Rolling Thunder, until the end of 1965, seven F-8C, -D, and -E squadrons from the *Bon Homme Richard*, *Ticonderoga*, *Midway*, and *Oriskany* engaged in combat operations. From their numbers, seven Crusaders were taken down by ground fire, two of those pilots surviving to become prisoners of the North Vietnamese.

North Vietnam's introductionof the Soviet Fire Can radar direction for 57-mm and 85-mm guns during that first year of Rolling Thunder made large-caliber antiaircraft artillery twice as effective in range and accuracy. (Designations and nicknames of Soviet-supplied systems were assigned by Western intelligence.) The more accurate gunfire forced alpha strikes to higher altitudes, where surface-to-air missiles (SAMs) became the predominant threat. In April 1965, just one month into Rolling Thunder, the presence of a Soviet-supplied SA-2 surface-to-air missile site under construction was confirmed by an RF-8A of VFP-63 Det D from the *Coral Sea*. By the end of 1965 more than sixty SA-2 sites were operational, from Hanoi to Haiphong. SA-2s were controlled by Spoon Rest acquisition radar and Fan Song guidance.

F-8s entered Rolling Thunder lacking any inherent ability to protect themselves electronically. Their best and really only protection, other than hard maneuvering, was that provided by standoff "electric" Skywarrior EA-3s along ingress and egress corridors. A crash program was instituted at the Bureau of Weapons (later, Naval Air Systems Command) to define a clap-on suite of avionics for at least limited electronic self-defense of carrier-based strike aircraft. Project Shoehorn, so-named because the added avionics had necessarily to be squeezed into existing space, assembled a suite of protective gear for F-8s that included

- An AN/ALQ-27 Sperry multiband automatic jamming system
- An AN/ALE-29 Tracor chaff and flare dispenser
- An AN/ALQ-51 Sanders deception jammer
- An AN/APR-27 Sanders radar-warning receiver
- An AN/ALR-27 Magnavox SAM-launch warning set.

F-8Cs and F-8Es with the retrofitted ALQ-51 equipment as part of suites of black boxes were readily identifiable by a fairing at the top of the vertical tail.

New electronic-countermeasures equipment amounted to so much dead weight without tactics to employ it. The task of developing the tactics fell to Air Test and Evaluation Squadron 4 at NAS Point Mugu, California. One of the project pilots assigned, Mike Welch, recalled tactics that were developed over not Ventura County, California, but Nashua, New Hampshire, where Sanders had reverse-engineered a simulator for the Fan Song. By the time he returned to the Vietnam theater flying F-8Es with VF-191, Welch was very familiar with the characteristic aural tones of the radar warning receiver: a low warbling sound indicating a Fan Song search, often followed by a higher-pitch chirping that indicated a lock-on. If the SA-2 missile could be spotted visually—a long telephone pole glowing red at one end—on its way toward your Crusader, you took evasive action, a dive away, and activated the ALE-29 to leave behind a ball of distracting chaff.[1]

AIR ORDER OF BATTLE

Complicating the threat picture was the presence of MiGs. Here, though, was something the Crusader community was predisposed by temperament and training to deal with, and if the F-8 itself was optimized for a particular mission, it was aerial combat with and dominance over MiGs. Prior to the start of Rolling Thunder in 1965, North Vietnam's fighter force had consisted of 36 MiG-17s sent in just after Pierce Arrow. During 1965, the Soviet Union supplied 80 MiG-21Ds and -21Fs, and the People's Republic of China continued shipments of MiG-17s.[2]

By September 1968 the North's inventory amounted to 153 MiGs, including 38 MiG-21s (Fishbeds), though many of the latter MiG-21s were repositioned away from Hanoi once American air forces were finally permitted to attack directly MiG airfields: Kep in April 1967 and Phuc Yen in October. North Vietnamese command and control from Bach Mai airfield continued relatively unscathed until late in the war. Operating initially from Phuc Yen then also Kep, MiG pilots were closely tied to the air-defense network through and their ground controllers in Bach Mai. When the network was alerted to the approach of a U.S. formation it picked the time, location, and direction of intercept that would best set up MiG pilots for a slashing attack, delivered diving past the target, after which he would retire to the sanctuary of one of the MiG airfields. It worked to the advantage of the North Vietnamese controllers and thus the MiG interceptors that U.S. Navy alpha strike groups repeatedly followed consistent—and predictable—courses and altitudes into North Vietnam and in recognizable formation patterns and at familiar airspeeds.

The MiG-17F, the predominant MiG type initially, presented nothing in firepower that had not been seen in the MiG-15 in Korea fifteen years before. Behind gunports recessed from the left-hand inlet lip were two Nudelman-Rikhter NR-23 (i.e., 23-mm) cannons and from the right-hand bay a single Nudelman N-37 cannon. The only real update over the MiG-15 was the Scan Fix (a NATO codename) radar that provided range data to the gunsight. The Scan Fix was believed to have been reversed-engineered from the U.S. APG-30 obtained from a captured F-86 that had crash-landed in Korea. It could detect targets at between three and four miles, alerting the cockpit with a buzzer; it did not make range data available until closing to about 1.5 miles.

The pilot could select 23-mm or 37-mm independently, but the MiG-17F did not carry an abundance of ammunition for either. Holding the trigger down would give the MiG pilot just over six seconds of 23-mm fire from the two guns or five-and-a-half seconds of 37-mm fire. However, a two-second burst from all cannons at once would send almost twice the projectile mass toward the enemy's airplane than the F-8's 20-mm guns could when all were firing. However, the MiG-17F pilot had to accept that firing his 23-mm and 37-mm together would mean that not all rounds would arrive at the aimpoint simultaneously, desirable for maximum lethality; the 23-mm and 37-mm had different ballistic flight paths, due to their different masses, and had different firing rates. The preferred option was apparently to fire one or the other.

The first MiG-21s to arrive in North Vietnam were -21F-13 Fishbed Cs in late 1965. These were followed by MiG-21PF Fishbed D variants in early 1966. Fishbed Cs were equipped with a single Nudel-Rikhter NR-30 (30-mm) cannon with a magazine holding up to sixty rounds. Pylons carried two AA-2 Atoll infrared (IR)–seeking missiles, one on each side; Atoll was reverse-engineered from a captured U.S. Sidewinder used by the Nationalist Chinese years before. "These first arriving -21F-13 models featured a range-only SRD-5ND radar that operated in two modes: for guns in one mode, it fed relative target speed and range out to 0.6 miles to an ASP optical gunsight, and alternately for missile firing in the other mode, range out to 1.4 miles for display on a firing range indicator."[3] Fishbed Ds did not initially carry an internal gun, only later acquiring a centerline cannon pod. Until then, Ds were equipped only with two Atoll IR missiles and with an improved RP-21 radar for limited all-weather capability.

The North Vietnamese were initially dissatisfied with the exchange rate experienced by their MiG-21s. In late 1967 that dissatisfaction resulted in a change in tactics. Whereas in early engagements MiG-21s had been scrambled to engage in turning combat with F-8s and other U.S. fighters below 15,000 feet, their tactics evolved throughout the last years of Rolling Thunder. Always under ground-based control until making their intercepts, MiG-21s were at that point more likely to be set up in pairs behind the U.S. strike aircraft formation and at higher altitude for an increase in speed when diving in the slashing attack, relying on flank attacks from MiG-17s at lower altitude to distract F-8 fighter escorts. A third MiG-21 would often trail behind the first two by two or three miles to engage American fighters that began to attack the first two MiG-21s.[4] For his part, the F-8 pilot could select the top two or bottom two 20-mm guns on each side independently or fire all four simultaneously. Holding the trigger down on all four guns would run him out of ammo in a dozen seconds, which mean more capacity for more short bursts of fire than the MiG-17F.

With F-8Cs, Ds, and Es in different squadrons during the campaign, there were as many different radar configurations. The F-8C was configured with AN/APS-67, which, when functioning properly, continuously scanned a pie-shaped section ahead of the aircraft out to 16 miles. The radar worked in conjunction with the EX-16 fire-control system, which consolidated airspeed, target range, angle rate, and 20-mm ballistic characteristics. The F-8D mounted an improvement with the AN/APQ-83 fire-control radar and an AN/AAS-15 infrared scanner mounted just forward of the front windscreen for target identification after acquisition. The AN/APQ-94 in the F-8E provided range and angle tracking out to 60 miles, with a 40-mile lock-on, when fully functional.[5]

F-8 pilots most often used fire control radar for joining strike formations and finding the tanker for refueling. Over the North Vietnam landscape, F-8 pilots normally depended rather on their own visual scan outside the cockpit and on calls from ship-based "Red Crown" controllers for intercept headings to get in position for stern shots with Sidewinders. As for their guns, experience had taught Crusader pilots that guns were prone to jam in high-g maneuvering. Up to December 1966, the guns either jammed or failed to fire at all "during three of the eight" times they were used against MiGs.[6] Normally the guns could be counted on only when very minimal or no g forces were being applied to the airframe. In fact, nearing the end of Rolling Thunder, the F-8 Tactical Manual strongly endorsed a "missile-first" doctrine: "AIM-9D [Sidewinder] should be considered the primary weapon unless the tactical situation dictates otherwise. This is not necessarily true for AIM-9B."[7]

The AIM-9B and -9D were the two Sidewinder models used most frequently in the early stages of the Vietnam air war, the AIM-9D appearing in numbers by 1967. The AIM-9B had at least a limited capability against targets maneuvering at up to 3 g's if launched within 25-degree "angle off"—that is, the two aircraft's headings diverging by no more than 25 degrees. However, the missile could not be counted on if the target was maneuvering at high g—the situation most likely to be encountered. The AIM-9D model, compared to the -9B, had nearly 0.7 Mach greater speed; a heftier, expanding-rod warhead; larger fins; and a nitrogen-cooled IR seeker for much-improved heat tracking. The remaining Sidewinder model was the AIM-9C, with semiactive radar homing to give the F-8 an all-weather radar-guided capability nearly equal to that of the longer-range AIM-7 Sparrow. The -9C sometimes found a place in a four-missile loadout but was used only sparingly in the theater and never scored in an air-to-air engagement.

Cdr. Hal Marr, a native of Oregon drawn into naval aviation from the enlisted ranks through the Flying Midshipman program, commanded VF-211 through its first three MiG kills, the first by Navy F-8s in the Vietnam air war, in 1966. (NNAM)

FIRST ENCOUNTERS

The first F-8/MiG-17 encounter occurred only weeks after Rolling Thunder got under way, and it came as a bit of a surprise. Navy aircraft were targeting a major highway bridge outside Thanh Hóa in the southern part of North Vietnam. Four F-8Es from VF-211 off the USS *Hancock* were out in front of the A-4s, having just pulled up from a flak-suppression run against antiaircraft artillery emplacements on the riverbank. Six MiG-17F-13s popped up from low altitude and singled out the two leading F-8Es, coming off the target. Lt. Cdr. Spence Thomas's F-8, in the lead, was damaged; hits to his utility hydraulic system would probably have prevented raising his wing for shipboard landing. He diverted to Da Nang and its 10,000-foot runway. The North Vietnamese, whose claims were often inflated, awarded credit to their pilot for a Crusader kill, based on fuzzy gunsight footage—the first "kill" for the Vietnam People's Air Force. Such as it is, the day, 3 April 1965, has been celebrated since in Vietnam in its commemoration.

More than fifteen months after Rolling Thunder officially "got rolling," Hal Marr, commanding VF-211, scored the first F-8 shootdown of a MiG-17. Marr was leading a section of VF-211 F-8Es and another of VF-24 F-8Cs providing "top cover" for a strike by eight A-4s of VA-212 and VA-216 on a military barracks complex 24 miles northwest of Haiphong. On Yankee Station in the *Hancock* for more than three months, the Crusader squadrons had grown frustrated at the lack of MiGs. The A-4 bombers, as the MiGs' primary targets, did not seem to lack for encounters, but the Crusaders seemed to be always out of position to "get a tally on"—to see—MiGs called out by the A-4s. Marr recalled his CAG, Cdr. Jack Monger, saying that "instead of spreading out our fighters in classic style, we'd stuff them right up with the strike group." On 12 June, "we were knee-deep in MiGs."[8]

Marr and his wingman, Lt. Phil Vampatella, once clear of SAMs, stepped up to 5,000 feet over the egressing A-4s when the MiGs appeared from the east

In June 1966 Hal Marr became the first Navy pilot to down a MiG in combat. Leading a flight of four Crusaders escorting eight A-4s, Marr turned his section on to four MiG-17s that were closing from behind at low altitude. Marr fired two AIM-9Ds that failed to guide due to high angle-off and high g loads. Marr then fired his two remaining AIM-9Ds, one of which tracked perfectly up the tailpipe of the trailing MiG and sliced the tail off. Here, he is congratulated upon his return to the USS *Hancock* in the squadron ready room. Lt. Cdr. Cole Black, standing at right, would be shot down nine days later and held in captivity in Hanoi until 1973. (NNAM)

at the seven o'clock position, very low. The MiG-17s were in pairs, their sections separated by 1,500 feet, when Marr called a turn to lead his F-8s into a head-on engagement. The MiGs started into a series of 360-degree turns, as Marr led his section into a series of "high yo-yo" maneuvers, slowing the closure rate to preserve "energy" (combining kinetic and potential energy and aircraft weight), while getting inside the MiGs' turns. The MiGs split up, with two vs. Marr's two F-8s and the others maneuvering out of sight. Marr squeezed off his first and second AIM-9D but with too much angle-off for the Sidewinders to track the target. As the MiGs came out of their turn to escape to the west, they committed a fatal error: they presented the pursuing F-8 with less g and less angle-off, giving the Sidewinder an easier tracking solution. Marr fired off his remaining two Sidewinders. One tracked up the lead MiG's tailpipe and tore off the tail, the MiG crashing near a river below. By this time Marr had lost sight of the rest of his F-8s and made his way alone out over the Tonkin Gulf. "Like many of his contemporary fighter squadron commanders, Marr emphasized the inclusion of dog fight training at the end of every training mission during their stateside training respites. The importance of stressing the combat bottom line in every aspect of their training was understood by Marr, White and Speer, his predecessor and successor, respectively, in command of VF-211."[9] The dogfighting ethos lived on!

On this, Air Wing 21's second combat cruise aboard the *Hancock*, remaining on Yankee Station into the early summer brought some improvement from monsoon weather. With that, alpha strikes were stepped up in areas still well outside the urban limits of Hanoi and Haiphong but now with more air opposition. As opposition intensified, so too did opportunity for F-8 squadrons to notch more victories in aerial combat. Just nine days after Marr's first MiG shootdown, two of his VF-211 pilots, Lieutenant (junior grade) Vampatella and Lt. Gene Chancy, each vanquished a MiG-17. That October Cdr. Richard Bellinger of VF-162 flying an F-8E from the *Oriskany* scored the first Crusader victory over a MiG-21.

A BANNER DAY

During the wing's third combat cruise, in 1967 aboard the *Bon Homme Richard*, large-scale alpha strikes entered a more aggressive stage. Increased exposure over North Vietnam brought, as a rule, more MiG opposition. The 19th day of May was fateful, and not just because it was a day of celebration in North Vietnam, Ho Chi Minh's birthday. A new targeting doctrine and a new weapon were making their debuts, and Air Wing 21 was selected to bring both to bear. In the first strike planned in downtown Hanoi, the AGM-62 Walleye would destroy Hanoi's thermal power plant and plunge the city into darkness for at least a few weeks. Walleye was a fire-and-forget TV-guided weapon that homed

Lethality	F-8E		MiG-17F
Guns	4 x 20 mm		1 x 37 mm + 2 x 27 mm
Magazine	125 rds/ea.		23mm = 80 rnds/ea. 37mm = 40 rnds
Rate-of-Fire	1,000 rnds/min		23mm = 870 rnds/min 37mm = 410 rnds/ min
Projectile Mass (2 sec Burst)	466 oz.		715 oz.
Detect & Track Limitations	AN/APQ-94 • Detection & Track ≤ 30 nm • Lock-On At 20-25 nm • Radar Rarely Used In-Country; Red Crown-Guided Intercept		SRC-3 "Scan Fix" • Gunsight Ranging Only • GCI-Guided Intercept To Rear Quarter Gun Solution
Accuracy Limitations	• Incorrect Sight Lead > 3g • Poor Readability of Mk12	VS.	• Different Ballistic Flight Path For 23mm & 37mm Projectiles • Excessive Gunsight Tracking Time For Lead Computation • Large Lead Required For Low Muzzle Velocity And Mass
Missiles	4 x AIM-9D IR Sidewinder		
Engagement Envelope**	Max Launch = 2.3nm Min Launch = 0.1nm Co-Speed (0.8M)/Co-Altitude (5k') 3g Turn/ < 30˚Angle-Off		
Visibility	Marginal Rear Quarter		Poor Over Canopy Rail
Survivability ① Airframe ② Pilot	① Mod-High Vulnerability To Gun & Missile Hits ② MB Mk5 Ejection Seat • Ballistic Catapult • Aero Stablized • Leg Restraints		① High Airframe Vulnerability To Missile Hits ② KK-2 Ejection Seat • Ballistic Catapult • Aero Stablized • Armored Seat/Cockpit

**based on specific engagement parameters

In measures of lethality, the F-8E entered an engagement with the MiG-17F with a slight advantage. In any engagement, other factors such as initial setup, altitude and speed difference, weapons and fuel remaining, tactics, training, experience, and aggressiveness shaped the outcome of the encounter. (*F-8e Aircraft Natops Flight Manual*, 15 January 1967; *F-8 Tactical Manual*, 15 June 1970; *Air-to-Air Encounters In Southeast Asia*, Ida, October 1967; Cia, *MiG-17 Characteristics*, 20 June 1957; Aircraft Illustrations, ©Jim Laurier, www.jimlaurier.com)

Members of VF-211 aboard the *Hancock*. Commanding officer Hal Marr stands sixth from left with his arm around the squadron mannequin mascot, "Ms. Checkmate." Two other squadron pilots would score MiG-17 shootdowns on this cruise: Lt. (jg) Phil Vampatella (kneeling, third from left) downed a MiG-17 on 21 June, and Lt. Gene Chancy (kneeling, fifth from left) downed a MiG-17 on the same mission. (Karen Black)

A veteran of the Korean War as a naval aviator, Cdr. Dick Bellinger was known by many as a colorful character with an infectious enthusiasm for aerial combat. After chasing a MiG-17 at rooftop level over the Hanoi suburbs in July 1966, Bellinger's F-8 took hits that knocked out the fuel probe. Unable to make the *Oriskany* without refueling, he ejected off the coast and was rescued by helicopter. (NNAM)

On 9 October 1966, three months after being shot down and rescued, Commander Bellinger was leading a flight of four F-8Es escorting an alpha strike into North Vietnam. Alerted to multiple unidentified bogies, Bellinger's flight was vectored to engage them. Bellinger followed a MiG-21 into a low-altitude "split-S" maneuver. With his F-8 inverted and 20 degrees nose-down, he fired two AIM-9D Sidewinders, rolling out as one of the missiles detonated close aboard the MiG. Bellinger (re-enacting the engagement with raised hand) became the first Navy pilot to shoot down a MiG-21 and for it would be awarded the Silver Star. (NNAM)

Lethality	F-8E		MiG-21F-13
Guns	4 x 20 mm		1 x 30 mm
Magazine	125 rds/ea.		60 rnds
Rate-of-Fire	1,000 rnds/min		850 rnds/min
Projectile Mass (2 sec Burst)	466 oz.		396 oz.
Detect & Track Limitations	AN/APQ-94 • Detection & Track ≤ 30 nm • Lock-On At 20-25 nm • Radar Rarely Used In-Country; Red Crown-Guided Intercept		SRD-5M "High Fix" • Gunsight Ranging Only • GCI-Guided Intercept To Rear Quarter Gun Solution
Accuracy Limitations	• Incorrect Sight Lead > 3g • Poor Readability of Mk12	vs.	• Gyro Drift When > 2g • Pipper Jetter Excessive
Missiles	4 x AIM-9D IR Sidewinder		2 x AA-2 IR "Atoll"
Engagement Envelope**	Max Launch = 2.3nm Min Launch = 0.1nm Co-Speed (0.8M)/Co-Altitude (5k') 3g Turn/ < 30°Angle-Off		Max Launch = 0.8nm Min Launch = 0.3nm Co-Speed (0.8M)/Co-Altitude (5k') 3g Turn/ < 25°Angle-Off (Gimbal Limit)*
Visibility	Marginal Rear Quarter		Poor Rear & Fwd Quarter Viz
Survivability ① Airframe ② Pilot	① Mod-High Vulnerability To Gun & Missile Hits ② MB Mk5 Ejection Seat • Ballistic Catapult • Aero Stablized • Leg Restraints		① High Vulnerability To Missile Hits ② KM-1 Ejection Seat • Rocket Boost/Aero Stabilized • Leg/Arm Restraints • Armored Seat/Cockpit

*estimated from AIM-9B performance

Lethality comparison of F-8E vs. MiG-21F-13: The MiG-21, a more capable adversary than the MiG-17 when flown to its potential, introduced an air-to-air missile into the mix. The Atoll missile was a copy of an earlier U.S. AIM-9B and was not as capable as the standard missile carried on the F-8E, the AIM-9D. Here too, as in comparison to the MiG-17, advantage can be influenced by numerous factors. (*F-8E Aircraft Natops Flight Manual*, 15 January 1967; *F-8 Tactical Manual*, 1 July 1969; Cia, *MiG-17 Characteristics*, 20 February 1959; Dia, *Have Doughnut: Tactical*, 1 August 1969; Aircraft Illustrations, ©Jim Laurier, www.jimlaurier.com)

VF-24 F-8Cs and VF-211 F-8Es assigned to Air Wing 21 position for launch from the USS *Bon Homme Richard* to join an alpha strike against targets in North Vietnam in March 1967. Note on the two F-8Es, on the port side (or far left) of the flight deck, the addition of the defensive electronic countermeasures suite fielded under Project Shoehorn; the ALQ-51 antenna is visible on the upper vertical tail. (Lawson Coll., Buehler Naval Aviation Library, NNAM)

on target contrast. Two A-4Es of VA-212 each flew with a Walleye, squadron commander Homer Smith in the lead and Lt. Cdr. Mike Cater flying wing. It was a departure of sorts from the usual alpha strike of twelve or more bomb-toting Skyhawks. Also, because of its significance, diversionary attacks were to be made at other North Vietnamese targets by groups from the *Kitty Hawk* and *Enterprise*. Several A-4Cs from VA-76 flew ahead as "Iron Hand," to destroy SAM sites. The mission profile took the flight west of Hanoi so that the sun was behind them on their approach. In addition to the visual difficulty the afternoon sun gave defenders, it maximized contrast to help the Walleye's sensor discriminate its target.

Surrounding the A-4s were twelve F-8s. VF-24's skipper, Cdr. Joe Ellison, led six F-8Cs in the van as flak suppressors, each armed with one AIM-9D Sidewinder and three Zunis. Among the six flak suppressors were Lt. Bobby Lee and his wingman Lt. (jg) Kit Smith. Cdr. Paul Speer, commander of VF-211, led a mix of F-8Es and F-8Cs, the F-8Es loaded with two AIM-9Cs on the port pylons—anticipating a possible longer-range, radar-guided, nose-on shot during ingress—and AIM-9Ds on the starboard pylons, per VF-211 squadron policy, and the F-8Cs loaded with four AIM-9D Sidewinders as escorts for the A-4s. Speer flew on the left flank with his wingman, Lt. (jg) Joe Shea. On the right flank were Lt. Cdr. Kay Russell and his wingman, Lt. (jg) Billy Foster, and half a mile to the rear of the A-4s was a VF-24 section led by Lt. Phil Wood, with Lt. (jg) Bill Metzger on his wing. Given the significance of this strike, Speer had decided to bring his escort fighters in closer than usual to the A-4s and match them in speed and altitude, rather than zigzagging overhead as normally done to keep airspeed up. He reasoned that North Vietnamese radar operators might well interpret the approaching group as a flight of unescorted Air Force F-105 Thunderchiefs (known by their crews as "Thuds") on their usual heading from the west over "Thud Ridge" (the Tam Dao Mountains, used as a waypoint). This might be all the spoofing needed to flush MiGs into the air from Kep and Phuc Yen to become targets themselves.[10]

After launch at 2 p.m. and join-up enroute, the strike group "went feet dry" (crossed the beach bound inland) south of Than Hoa heading northwest and hugging the side of the Tu Le hills to minimize exposure to ground radar. When the aircraft turned east toward Hanoi, the Red River plain opened up, the last ten miles to the power plant. Almost immediately, Lee called out a MiG-17 that was chasing an A-6 from one of the diversionary strikes. Wood gave chase with Metzger in tow, fired a Sidewinder but outside the maneuvering envelope of the missile, which failed to guide. The MiG unloaded, "dove for the deck" and escaped at high speed up a narrow valley. Wood chased it far enough to ensure that it wouldn't be an immediate threat to the A-4s, then tried to catch up to his strike group. Well out in front of his Crusader, the strike group had reached the target area and to Wood it appeared as if "all hell had broken loose . . . black and gray puffs of 57mm and 85mm anti-aircraft artillery, air-to-air missile trails, white streamers of SA-2 SAMs lifting off their pads and silver MiGs," a colorful tableau of highly lethal aerial warfare.[11]

Lieutenant Lee, with his flak suppressors approaching a lake just west of the power plant, grew annoyed by the incessant growl of his ALR-27 gear. Numerous SA-2 Spoon Rest radars spread out below were actively tracking the flight. He took his wingman, Kit Smith, down below 400 feet to lessen some of the aural distraction and then, approaching his initial point (which set his two-plane section up for a planned attack run on an SA-2 site), pulled up to 3,000 feet, rolled upside down to pull his nose down on the target keeping positive g's on the airplane, and unleashed his Zunis; his wingman did the same. As they pulled out from their run a MiG-17 crossed directly in front of them. Lee leveled off at 700 feet and selected a Sidewinder, while trying to turn with the MiG. He detected the aural tone from the missile seeker that indicated lock-on, but the missile when fired flew out of sight to the outside of his turn. Thinking his Sidewinder had failed to make the turn, he was surprised to see it cross back in front of him and snake directly into the MiG between its wing trailing edge and tail. The MiG's tail section rotated toward the outside of the turn as it separated from the fuselage.

Phil Wood, meanwhile, was regaining position on his strike group when he realized that his wingman was nowhere in sight. He first heard the crack, then the sight, of 37-mm tracers zipping by his canopy. He pulled

On their third combat cruise, this time aboard the USS *Bon Homme Richard*, VF-211 upped its tally of MiGs. Lt. Cdr. Mo Wright (*standing, seventh from left*) downed a MiG-17 on 1 May 1967. Paul Speer (*standing, fifth from left*), who relieved Hal Marr as commanding officer, downed a MiG-17 on 19 May. Lt. (jg) Joseph Shea (*kneeling, third from right*) downed his MiG-17 on the same mission, as Speer's wingman. Lt. Tim Hubbard (*standing, second from left*) scored his MiG-17 kill on 21 July 1967. (Vern Larson)

hard left and could see the MiG 1,000 feet behind at his seven o'clock position. Holding g's on his airplane in the turn, he could see the MiG's angle-off increasing. The MiG pilot was likely new to the fight and rather than attempting to hold the Crusader in a Lufbery-like circle (see chapter 4) to drain off airspeed and gain a turn-rate advantage, committed his fatal error: he reversed his turn, unintentionally setting up a shot for Wood. Wood switched his armament and got a strong tone from the selected AIM-9D seeker head. The missile left the rail, appeared to drop ballistically, then began a climb, tracking the MiG's tailpipe, and severed the entire empennage. The forward end of the MiG pitched over, slowed, and the pilot ejected. Wood passed the pilot close enough, he later said, to distinguish unit patches on his flight suit. The MiG pilot separated from his seat but his main chute streamed, failed to open properly, and he did not survive impact with the field below. Wood joined on squadron commander Speer going feet wet, not yet aware that his wingman Metzger had been shot down. Nor was he aware that Speer had just taken his own MiG-17.

VF-211's commanding officer, Cdr. Paul Speer (*left*), reviews the mission just flown with his wingman, Joe Shea. Each had shot down a MiG-17F earlier that day while escorting a strike on a Hanoi power plant, 19 May 1967. (NNAM)

Wood had been still chasing his first MiG when the two A-4s arrived at their initial point, pitched up to 4,000 feet, and delivered their Walleyes. Speer put his remaining escort F-8s in burner and led them zooming up to 6,000 feet to cover the A-4s' egress over the Hanoi suburbs. Speer scanned left and caught the flash of an upturned wing as a MiG-17 began pulling toward him. Instinctively pulling toward the MiG, he made a series of twisting "scissors turns," hoping to make the MiG overshoot ahead of him. Pirouetting through five or six scissors turns at high g and in afterburner, he realized that his best shot from this close would be with the AIM-9Ds on his right-wing rails. But his armament-select switch was still to the left, where only AIM-9Cs waited. Holding the MiG in sight throughout the scissors maneuvering, he was able to reach against the g forces to select his right-hand AIM-9Ds, and the aural growl of the Sidewinder sensor registered immediately. Inexplicably, like his compatriot, the MiG pilot reversed. Speer fired, but inside the effective range of the missile and still with such high g's on his airplane that the Sidewinder could not make the turn. The MiG, in his last questionable move, then unloaded, relaxing g's on his airplane to build up speed and make his escape. Speer saw it and fired his second (and final) AIM-9D. The Sidewinder guided to the MiG's empennage and detonated in a bright flash. The MiG appeared to fly on, even as debris flew off the airplane. In seconds, flames consumed the rear end of the MiG and it tumbled to impact on the ground.

Paul Speer's one-on-one combat over, he rejoined the strike group with his Joe Shea at Speer's five o'clock position about 1,000 feet away. Just as the pair was catching up to the A-4s, another MiG-17 flew right between Speer and Shea in hot pursuit of one of the A-4s. The MiG veered right after the turning A-4; Speer lost sight of him, and Shea took the lead. Shea pulled hard right to set up a 20-mm

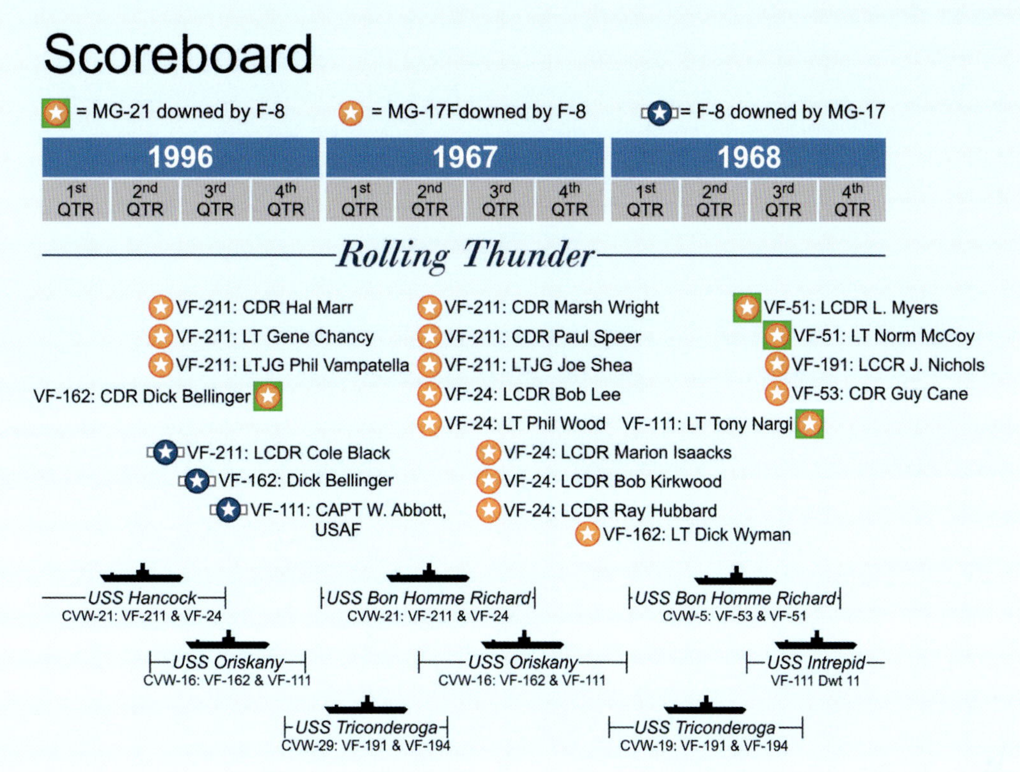

After a first year of limited aerial engagements for Navy F-8s in Rolling Thunder, things intensified in 1966. Four MiGs were downed by F-8s, for the loss of three F-8s. By the next year, deploying F-8 squadrons were dominating in their MiG encounters, largely due to better understanding and anticipation of MiG tactics and employment of counter tactics. Overall in Rolling Thunder, the loss of three F-8s was offset by 18 MiG kills, yielding a six-to-one exchange rate. Most MiG kills were by Sidewinders; at best, two were gun shootdowns, and guns contributed in two more kills. (Evans and Grossnick, *United States Naval Aviation 1910–2010*, Vol. 2, Chap. 38, 463; graphic by Ernest Snowden)

tracking solution, then fired. His primary concern was to get the MiG to break off the attack on the A-4 once its pilot saw tracers over his canopy. It worked. The MiG broke left, and Shea continued firing as he closed to within 700 feet. Now it appeared that a missile shot might work. Shea's Sidewinder left its rail, flew through his own 20-mm fire, and detonated just behind the MiG. The MiG immediately pitched nose-over and hit the ground no more than 200 feet below Shea.[12]

Reportedly, sixteen MiG-17s rose from Kep and Phuc Yen airfields that afternoon. In a total elapsed time of no more than six minutes, Navy F-8s took down four of them, a one-day tally that would not be met or exceeded by Navy fighters until five years later when Navy F-4s claimed eight MiGs. The elation within the air wing was tempered by the realization that two F-8s, flown by Lieutenant (junior grade) Metzger of VF-24 and Lt. Cdr. Russell of VF-211, had been shot down. Also, results of the Walleye drops were less than encouraging. The A-4 pilots reported that one weapon went long and hit the far end of the power plant and the other just short of the generator hall.[13]

Two days later a second visit was paid on the Hanoi power plant, this time by four A-4s carrying Walleyes, escorted by another group of F-8s from VF-211 and VF-24. Battle-damage assessment determined that one or more Walleyes had caved in the boiler-house roof and that one or more flattened the generator hall. No MiGs were reported shot down.[14]

Two months later, on 21 July, Air Wing 21 was again over North Vietnam, and Crusaders from VF-211 and VF-24 were flying combat air patrol for A-4s hitting petroleum storage tanks at Ta Xa, twenty miles north of Haiphong. Three more MiG-17s fell. Lt. Cdr. Marion Isaacks claimed the first with a Sidewinder. Lt. Cdr. Ray Hubbard accounted for a second with a combination of guns and Zuni rockets. Lt. Cdr. Bob Kirkwood scored his MiG-17 kill with his 20-mm cannons, the only occasion where a Navy fighter claimed a shootdown using only guns. This was the next-highest single-day tally of MiG kills scored by Navy F-8s.

Nevertheless, guns played a vital part in all encounters, whether or not credited for shootdowns. Though records show that guns jammed or did not fire at all in three of eight engagements involving 20-mm firings in one particular year, the "opportunity space" created by setting up a gun solution could be leveraged for another weapon. Gunnery was embodied in the training and mindset of Crusader pilots maneuvering to obtain the best shooting option. Adm. Paul Gillcrist described it best: "[A]lthough the gun never killed many MiGs in the southeast Asian air war, having it was critical. The deadliest tactic was always to maneuver aggressively for a gun kill. While so doing, the Crusader pilot usually passed through the heart of the envelope for a Sidewinder shot and took it. Having the gun enabled the Crusader pilot to stay aggressive throughout the engagement . . . and to stay alive!"[15] This complementary relationship was never more in evidence than when in June 1968 Cdr. Lowell Myers of VF-51 closed in on a MiG-21 in a low-level aerial duel. Reaching gun range, he fired several streams of 20-mm rounds with tracers. The sight of the tracers was enough to panic the MiG-21 pilot into pulling up, giving Myers' AIM-9D a distinctive heat contrast—afterburner against clear, blue sky—and Myers himself a strong seeker-head tone. His Sidewinder tracked into the MiG's tailpipe and exploded.[16]

MAKING IT LAST: REMANUFACTURE

In 1963 the Navy had in commission seven *Forrestal*- or later-class "supercarriers," as well as three *Midway*-class and five *Essex*-class carriers ordered during World War II and since converted to angled decks. Secretary of Defense Robert McNamara grudgingly supported an inventory of fifteen CVAs (his advisors argued for eight) but advocated a drawdown of the *Essex* and *Midway* classes through the late 1960s and early 1970s, to be replaced by new large carriers to reach thirteen.[17] As plainly demonstrated fifteen years earlier in the Korean War, once again the vital necessity for carrier airpower, this time in Vietnam, altered the force-structure calculus. As the conflict escalated, it was readily apparent that the planned peacetime CVA force was insufficient to maintain the required five attack carriers in the western Pacific. The *Essex*-class carriers were essential to the rotation of carrier air wings into the Gulf of Tonkin. However, size constrained the *Essex* class to the F-8 Crusader for its fighters; the F-4 was simply too large for efficient flight-deck handling. Transition of F-8 squadrons to F-4s would be delayed as long as the *Essex* carriers were needed to prosecute the air war.

By this point, the F-8 had been flown hard. Not just flight hours but carrier landings had taken a toll on the "fatigue life" of important structural components, especially wings, tailhooks, and landing gear. There being no planned life-extension program, indeed no whole-aircraft means of recording failures of high-time components, the Navy needed to remanufacture F-8s of the series most in demand. Disassembling the aircraft for remanufacture also presented opportunity for updating navigation and communication, fire control systems, electronic countermeasures (ECM), and avionics, which had not been upgraded in the F-8D, for example, in more than six years. Aircraft of each series were selected to be modified, in large part on the basis of fatigue life remaining:

Series	Quantity Modified	New Designation
RF-8A	73	RF-8G
F-8B	61	F-8L
F-8C	87	F-8K
F-8D	89	F-8H
F-8E	136	F-8J

Five photo reconnaissance RF-8As began Crusader modernization at the Vought plant in 1964 for partial conversions that added ventral fins and a new, stronger wing. Fifteen more were inducted into the program in 1965, with authorization for another fifty-three over the next two years. In addition to the ventral fins and the new 4,000-hour wing, with hard points for wing stores and fuel pods, these latter aircraft received fuselage structural reinforcements, a new molded-harness electrical system, and a new engine, the more powerful J57-P20. The new engine came with more electrical power, from a 20-kva generator. The increased electrical power made possible additional and better cameras, as well as electronic countermeasures systems identified by Project Shoehorn. The modernized RF-8As rolled off Vought's assembly line as RF-8Gs, the first getting airborne in August 1965.

Inducted right behind the RF-8Gs came the F-8Ds, in July 1967. The Ds received the same structural improvements as the RF-8Gs but also guidance equipment for the Bullpup missile. The guidance components were added to an area over the wing center

Lt. Elmer Gildersleeve, assistant catapult officer on the *Oriskany*, signals Lt. Robert Punches in the cockpit of a VF-162 F-8E about to launch for a mission over North Vietnam armed with four AIM-9D Sidewinders. This was *Oriskany's* third combat cruise. (NHHC)

section and blended in with the outer mold line by a fairing that gave the aircraft a distinctive hump. Other high-time, fatigue-limited structural components throughout the airplane were swapped out to match the 4,000-hour life of the wing. The modernized D model was redesignated F-8H.

Toward the end of the 1960s, 136 F-8Es began to receive the same changes that went into the remanufactured F-8H, including Bullpup control. The French navy's experience with F-8s led to the adoption in the Es' remanufacturing program of boundary-layer control (BLC), double leading-edge droops, and a decrease in wing incidence from seven degrees to five. The motivation was clearly to slow landing speeds and, it was reasoned, improve landing mishap statistics. Because the airplane with BLC approached more slowly, a larger "unit horizontal tail" was required to restore control. F-8Es emerged from remanufacture as F-8Js with a new and weightier ALQ-100 ECM suite, a new radar/fire-control setup with a somewhat heavier AN/APQ-124, and other changes that added an overall 2,000 pounds.

The increase in empty weight made the aircraft noticeably more sluggish in up-and-away performance. If BLC had an overriding problem it was that it required extra thrust on approach to compensate for the bleed air extracted from the engine to be blown over the aileron and flap—nearly 1,000 pounds of thrust not available for throttle corrections. An engine swap to the J57-P420 upped available thrust in military power by 1,500 pounds, which eased the thrust shortfall somewhat. Even though BLC reduced its landing speed by ten to fifteen knots, the J was considered a dangerous aircraft flown near the ship, especially at night. "Although the approach speeds were down around the 120-knot range at max trap weight, you couldn't see over the nose and wave-off capability was pathetic. To add to your worries, you could fly the airplane below the minimum speed for operation of the emergency ram air turbine. . . . [Y]ou could be on final at night, operating the RAT [ram air turbine] and then lose all electrical power."[18] Gradually, fixes were applied by adjusting flight control rigging, reworking the RAT, and, ultimately, replacing the engine with the P&W J57-P400 series for added thrust.

When not engaged in direct combat operations over North Vietnam, Crusader squadrons transiting to or from the Tonkin Gulf were frequently tasked with intercepting Russian interlopers. In 1967, after ending a third "line period" in the Gulf, a VF-162 F-8 intercepts a Russian Tu-95 Bear. (ALAMY)

The final remanufacture took the F-8B and F-8C to the F-8L and F-8K. The Ks received the ventral fins, whereas the Ls were fitted "for but not with" the fins. Other than the new 4,000-hour wing, modifications were more limited for the L and K series than for the H and J. The L and K series would take a less robust baseline capability into an upgrade, and overall inventory needs for the Crusader were rapidly declining. By the start of the next phase of intensive air warfare over North Vietnam in 1972, only three *Essex*-class carriers converted in what was known as the "27C" program were still in commission to host Crusader squadrons, and those were very near to decommissioning.

THE TALLY

Operations Linebacker I and II in 1972 signaled the resumption of punishing strikes into North Vietnam. Intended to roll back a North Vietnamese offensive into South Vietnam and force the North's regime into a negotiated settlement, the Linebacker campaigns resembled the alpha strikes of Rolling Thunder but made greater use of "smart" weapons for infrastructure reduction, latitude in targeting MiG bases, and the mining Haiphong Harbor. For Crusader squadrons they meant diminishing involvement, as fewer smaller-deck carriers deployed into the theater and remaining F-8 squadrons were successively reequipped with F-4 Phantom IIs. Four F-8 squadrons, all flying F-8Js, saw limited action in Linebacker: VF-24 and VF-211 of CVW-21 in the *Hancock* and VF-191 and VF-194 of CVW-19 in the *Oriskany*.

Considering the Vietnam air war as having two, distinct campaign phases, the Crusader effectiveness is more accurately gauged in terms of Rolling Thunder. The Crusader tally in that campaign was 18 MiGs shot down for a loss of 3 in aerial combat, yielding a kill rate of 6 to 1. By contrast, over the Rolling Thunder years Navy F-4s scored 14 shootdowns and lost 5 in aerial combat, for an exchange rate of 2.8 to 1. Losses to SA-2 SAMs in that period are similar: 10 for the F-8 and 11 for the F-4. For Marines in the South, three F-8 squadrons, in several rotations, suffered the loss of 22 aircraft, some to ground fire, more to operational causes.[19]

NOTES

1. Capt. J. Michael Welch, USN (Ret.), Interview by Ernest Snowden, 2 July 2024.

2. Central Intelligence Agency, Intelligence Directorate, "Sources of Military Equipment to Viet Cong and North Vietnamese Military Forces," 4 November 1968, accessed 15 June 2024 at https://www.cia.gov/readingroom/docs/DOC_0000381439.pdf.